The Desecration of Christ

The Desecration
of Christ

by RICHARD EGENTER

Translated by EDWARD QUINN

Edited by NICOLETE GRAY

FRANCISCAN HERALD PRESS
CHICAGO · ILLINOIS 60609

FRANCISCAN HERALD PRESS
1434 West Fifty-First Street, Chicago, Illinois 60609
First published in America 1967

This is a translation and adaptation of
Kitsch and Christenleben (*Buch-Kunstverlag Ettal*)
with an Epilogue by Nicolete Gray.

Printed in Great Britain
Bound in the U.S.A.

Contents

Chapter	Page
Editor's Foreword	9

Part One: WHAT IS KITSCH?
Introduction, p. 13—How can Kitsch be
recognized? p. 14.

I. AESTHETIC EXPERIENCE	17

The Experience of the Creative Artist, p. 17
—Form in Art, p. 21—What determines the
Value of a Work of Art? p. 23—Art as Communication, p. 25—The Response of the Beholder, Listener or Reader, p. 27.

II. ART AND MORALITY	31

The Artist and Morality, p. 31—Morality and
the Beholder, p. 36.

III. THE ORIGINS OF KITSCH	38

With the Artist, p. 38—The Origin of Kitsch
in the Viewer, p. 50—What then is Kitsch?
p. 53.

IV. KITSCH AND THE WORLD TODAY	55

Sentimentality, p. 55—Tendentiousness and
Propaganda in Kitsch, p. 58—Kitsch and
Modern Art, p. 60—Kitsch and the Man in
the Street, p. 62—Children and Kitsch, p. 67
—The Art-Historical Background, p. 68.

Chapter   Page

 V. THE BREEDING GROUND OF KITSCH AND ITS
    MORAL EFFECTS   74
       Original Sin, p. 74—Timidity and Emotional
       Immaturity, p. 75—Repressed Sex, p. 77—
       Religious Decadence, p. 78—Collectivization,
       p. 79—Unbalanced Extremes in the Under-
       standing of Art, p. 80—Self-indulgence, p. 84.

VI. MORAL INEPTITUDE AS THE HEART OF KITSCH   85
       Untruthfulness, Irreverence, Shamelessness,
       p. 85—The Devastating Effects of Kitsch,
       p. 90.

        Part Two: KITSCH IN CATHOLIC WORSHIP
                  AND MORALITY

 I. KITSCH IN THE CHURCH TODAY   95
       Liturgy, p. 95—Images of the Saints, p. 97—
       Popular Hymns, p. 99—Devotional Articles,
       p. 103—"Edifying" Literature, p. 104—
       Kitsch and the Priest, p. 104.

II. ART AND KITSCH IN RELIGION   107
       True Religious Art, p. 107—Lack of Religious
       Inspiration, p. 107—Types of Art and Types
       of Response, p. 109—A Summary, p. 112—
       Kitsch as a Danger to Religion, p. 114.

III. THE KITSCH IDEAL OF THE CHRISTIAN MAN   120

        Part Three: OVERCOMING KITSCH

 I. THE AESTHETIC APPROACH   129
       Clearing out the Rubbish, p. 130—Education,
       p. 130—A New Popular Art, p. 132.

II. THE MORAL APPROACH   137

    EPILOGUE: KITSCH IN ENGLAND TODAY   143

Illustrations

Between pages 96 and 97

1. A Saint. Carlo Dolci
2. A bunch of violets. Dürer. *Albertina, Vienna*
3. The Infant Jesus with St John and two Angels. Rubens. *Kunsthistorisches Museum, Vienna*
4. Jesus in the tabernacle. Modern German drawing, by a woman
5. The Gift of the Fear of the Lord. "Holy" card, printed in Italy
6. The Christ of St John of the Cross. Painting by Salvador Dali. *Glasgow Art Gallery and Museum*
7. The Sacrament of the Last Supper. Painting by Salvador Dali. *National Gallery of Art, Washington, D.C. Chester Dale Collection*
8. The Rest on the Flight into Egypt. Painting by Philip Veit
9. Mary as the Good Shepherdess. "Holy" card, German
10. The Infant Samuel. Painting by Reynolds. *Tate Gallery, London*
11. Baby Jesus. From a child's book printed in Italy
12. Our Lady. Card printed in England
13. The Penitent Magdalene
14. The Light of the World. Painting by Holman Hunt. *Keble College, Oxford*
15. Card of the Sacred Heart
16. Three typical German "holy" cards
17. Madonna and Child. Two medals. Widely available
18. Madonna. Statue by Feuchtmayr
19. Immaculata. Statue by Günter
20. Guardian angel. Card printed in Italy
21. Elijah, from Bible illustrated by Tissot (1902)
22. *Noli me tangere*, from Bible illustrated by Hole (1906)

7

23. *Noli me tangere*. Painting by Graham Sutherland. *Chichester Cathedral*
24. Illustration by Jacques le Scanff from *Joseph* (Dove Books, 1966)
25. St Anthony. Statue made in Italy
26. Crucifixion. Painting by Graham Sutherland. *Church of St Aidan, East Acton*
27. The raising of Lazarus. Stained glass by John Piper, made by Patrick Reyntiens. *Eton College Chapel*, 1958
28. The Risen Christ. Statue by Elizabeth Frink

Acknowledgements

Plate
14. Reproduced by permission of Keble College, Oxford
22. By permission of Eyre & Spottiswoode, Ltd
27. By permission of the artist
28. Central Press Photos, Ltd

Publisher's Note

THE word "kitsch" is untranslatable, and does actually now appear in the *Concise Oxford Dictionary*. A considerable part of this book is concerned with the discussion of its precise meaning, but for the reader who is not familiar with the word it may be taken as a starting-point to mean "repository art" and its counterpart in music, verse and the other arts. It is not by any means applied only to pious art, but this is the aspect with which this book is concerned. "Kitsch" is a noun which can be used adjectivally.

Editor's Foreword

PROFESSOR EGENTER'S book which is here translated is
the second edition of a work first published in 1958. It is
an attack by a moral theologian on the evil caused by
kitsch statues, paintings, hymns, writings, etc., not from
the point of view of aesthetic taste, but from the point of
view of the effects of kitsch on the moral and religious life
of German Catholics. This is a theme which also has an
undoubted reference to the life of the Catholic Church
elsewhere; many of our religious art-objects are German,
others are in international circulation among Catholics.
On the other hand there are of course differences between
the situation here and in Germany. Our tradition in religious art is quite different—we have indeed very little post-
Renaissance tradition—and to some extent we are familiar
with different paintings of the past from those current in
Germany. In particular German nineteenth-century art is
little known outside Germany; nor on the whole is German
literature or art criticism. We all share the common culture of the twentieth-century West, with its failings, but
there are differences in temperaments and in recent
history. For these reasons I was asked by Burns and Oates
to edit the book for English-speaking readers. I have therefore substituted other examples where I thought the
German were unfamiliar or irrelevant, and occasionally
added a sentence to bring out an English connection. The
number of illustrations of kitsch has also been increased, as
neither the concept nor the word are currently familiar

9

outside Germany. All the additional illustrations are marked and the commentaries on them in the text are of course mine. I have tried in every case to find examples which as far as possible illustrate the same point as that made by the author's original example.

This, as far as I know, will be the first book on kitsch to be published in England or the United States. Professor Egenter's book draws on a considerable body of earlier German literature—I believe that there is even a museum of kitsch in Stuttgart. But it seemed best, in order to make the main arguments of his thesis as clear as possible to an English-speaking readership, to omit those passages which were mainly directed to German readers. The result, therefore, is a considerably abridged version of the German edition. The text is based throughout on the translation made by Father Edward Quinn, but where a free translation seemed to make the author's meaning clearer I have used my own words.

For references to hymns and music, and in particular for the whole section "popular hymns" I am indebted to Father Laurence Bévenot, O.S.B.

Throughout, my overriding purpose has been to get the author's message across to the English public. It seems to me one of the utmost importance and urgency.

NICOLETE GRAY

Part One
WHAT IS KITSCH ?

Introduction

Is kitsch a sin? There can be no simple answer to such a question. It raises complicated issues which require careful analysis.

The question, Is kitsch a sin? may be countered with another: Is stupidity a sin? But one speaks of "criminal stupidity". There is also criminal kitsch.

The marriage between art and the Church is fruitful, but it has not always been happy. The Church has at various times found it necessary to oppose decadence in art. Art also sometimes has had to fight for the right to assert its true nature. It is a human activity willed by the Creator, with its own dignity and mission. When short-sighted pastoral zeal robs it of these essential qualities, then they must be vindicated; particularly when it is Christian truth and the fullness of Christian life which the art in question is expected to express.

It would therefore be disastrous if Christian ethics and pastoral theology refused to concern themselves with the problem of kitsch. It may seem a marginal consideration but if kitsch is allowed to persist, if we train ourselves not to notice the instances as they pile up, we are allowing it to create a scandal which drives people out of the Church, or deprives them of life within it. The argument of this book will perhaps make it clear that the Father of lies possesses in kitsch a wonderfully flexible and effective means of turning the masses away from salvation. The dominion of kitsch over Catholic life during the past century has been at times almost absolute; to what extent has this been responsible for the falling away of the masses from Christian life? In our own country, how many would be converts has it repulsed? Can we be sure that it plays no part in the lapse rate? No doubt during this period the whole question of the relation between art and a rapidly changing society has created general problems, but have there not also been sins of omission on the part of those who had eyes to see and did not see? Sometimes omissions and sins of omission are more dangerous than the most monstrous crimes.

Kitsch is not merely a question of taste, it strikes at man himself, his moral health and salvation. In this work the writer, being a moral theologian, will approach the subject from the standpoint of Christian ethics rather than from the aesthetic standpoint. However, the moral theologian must also deal with what is aesthetically significant, even though he cannot claim to pass judgment. His is the last word, but he must also welcome, and pay attention to, the evidence of artists and art historians.

How can Kitsch be recognized?

Sometimes an examination of a word and its derivation will elucidate its meaning. "Kitsch" is not derived from any German root. It has been suggested that it originated in Munich and comes from the English word "sketch" (*Skizze*), being used to describe the inferior artefacts made to please, or to take in, the nineteenth-century tourist. However that may be, kitsch has nothing to do with "sketch". A taste for kitsch is very often a taste for something complete in every detail.

How then can we tell what is kitsch? (It is translated in one dictionary as "shoddy, trash, tripe, slush, cheap sentimentality, hokum, sob-stuff"). It is best perhaps to start with a very cautious definition; a thing which is kitsch is "a work which in some way claims to belong to the realm of art but in this respect remains inadequate". As a definition even this is too wide, for there may be inadequacies in works of art, not excluding religious art, which have nothing to do with kitsch; in works which, for instance, are quite sincere, but weak, where the artist lacks talent, or depth of feeling—such inadequacies as these do not make kitsch. The inclusion of some relationship to art is, however, essential to a precise definition; kitsch is related to human experience in the form of the beautiful—beauty not necessarily in the sense of harmony, of what pleases the senses, but in the wider sense as the specific element in art, the element which can be present also in abstract art, or in an aesthetic expression of the horrifying, as in much Greek drama. The dictionary semi-synonyms need therefore this first qualification.

Kitsch is artistic miscarriage; but how can it be judged? By what characteristics, or upon what principles can it be distinguished? For instance, is a plaster or plastic cast painted to look like a Gothic wood-carving kitsch? If so it cannot be the material itself which makes it so—plaster casts used for study are not kitsch and plastic has a thousand excellent uses. Is it the element of deception in the painted replica which is wrong? Here perhaps is a clue. Let us take another example: a gaudily coloured picture postcard view is kitsch. Is that because of the subject chosen, or the cheap and crude type of reproduction? Crudity hardly seems to be a criterion, for many primitive works of art are crude without being kitsch. On the other hand, technical brilliance will not save an artist from fall-

ing into kitsch; painting such as Carlo Dolci's Saint (Plate
1) or Richard Wagner's song *The Angel* come perilously
near; the gifted artist is certainly not immune. Does the
kitsch lie perhaps in some lack of proper connection between words and music, in some lack of suitability between
the subject and its treatment? In extreme examples, where
a coquettish pious innocent is imposed on us as a saint, or
when our longing for heaven is served up in a sentimental
hymn there is no mistaking that there is a crass divergence
between what the artist claims to be expressing and what
is actually represented. Here we are surely nearer to the
heart of the matter, and in this case it would seem that the
roots of kitsch must lie somewhere in the creative, or
would-be creative experience of the artist—or in the
response of the beholder. If we are to arrive at a more
precise definition, if we are to understand the morally
disintegrating effect of kitsch, we must first briefly analyse
these two types of experience. It is clear that the diagnosis
is complex and delicate.

I

Aesthetic Experience

The Experience of the Creative Artist

WE speak of the creative activity. It would be more accurate to use the word "procreative". Art is begotten, not made. The artist experiences a tension which seeks release, and the fruit of this experience is a new entity; a new structure which cannot be excogitated, but which the artist accepts as a gift, a grace, which grows in him, and which he brings to birth, often painfully and arduously. It is characteristic of the artistic experience that it involves no direct gratification of instinct or purposive realization of talents. On the contrary, it is out of a deliberate renunciation of such immediate and actual satisfaction that works of art emerge; indeed they are often born out of suffering, when the artist finds himself confronted by an inner reality which he must pursue though it run counter to his own wishes and plans. (Not that the artist himself in the moment of creation needs to understand his own activity, or to watch over or analyse his own action; like procreation it is a mystery, a gift.) That which the artist receives in his moment of inspiration he transforms, clarifies, and deepens with the intensity of his feeling into an image of the mind. And out of this image, which is part of itself, his creative energy forms and moulds a work of art perceptible to sense.

But no artist living in the world of men works for himself alone; in his work he seeks not just self-expression, but communication with others. In the same way the complementary experience of looking at, reading, hearing a work of art, is not a cold, conceptual apprehension, but personal contact with its creator. That which came to the artist grew in him, compelled him to give it a shape, is transmitted by this sensible shape to the soul of the beholder and should there awaken and enrich his aesthetic sensibilities. For the beauty or power of a work of art cannot automatically arouse this response. Its full realization requires not only aesthetic perception (and people are unequally gifted with visual as well as musical percipience), but also some sort of understanding that goes deeper and further than the rational processes of the mind, and personal integrity. Without qualities in the beholder even a great work of art may be experienced as kitsch; kitsch may in fact originate in a personal or moral defect here as easily as in an aesthetic defect. But before examining this conclusion we have first to continue our consideration of the experience of the artist.

One day in April 1802, William Wordsworth and his sister went for a walk near Ullswater and came across a hillside covered with wild daffodils. As a result Wordsworth was moved to write a poem. Goethe also wrote a poem about a flower, a violet, which was one day read by Mozart. It enchanted him, filling his mind with thoughts of spring, which he turned into music. Dürer once saw the outstretched hand of a child clasping a bunch of violets and immortalized his memory of it in the watercolour which is now in the Albertina in Vienna (Plate 2).

In all these cases the first impact came to the artist from outside as an objective experience, their poetry and music was engendered, not created out of nothing; and this holds good also for absolute music and abstract painting. At the beginning is the chance encounter with some particular thing (such as a flower) awaking something in the creative mind, something which—possibly after a period of lying fallow—begins to live and grow and to become transformed into an inner image. Eventually it emerges in a new shape—as a picture or a poem, but in between it has been part of the artist's life. It does not remain isolated in his mind, it gathers to itself associations. Wordsworth in his poem on the daffodils thought of the stars, and the waves of the sea, and beyond, through the visual associations, to our sense of infinity, of joy and its expression in movement and dance, and then he changed from joy in what he saw, to joy in the memory of what he saw:

> They flash upon that inward eye
> Which is the bliss of solitude.

Is this inner image always a valid one? Or in what sense is it valid? The mind which experiences the initial impression is not a blank page. It is marked by innumerable earlier experiences. Not only this; each human nature has its own bent towards particular behaviour patterns which become explicit in the innate imagery of our minds. Jung speaks of archetypes. (The demonic shape and power which such innate imagery can assume we can see, for instance, in the paintings of Hieronymus Bosch or of Surrealists like Max Ernst.) In fact valid artistic expression is very rarely the simple record of an impression, not even with the French impressionists who set out to be scientifically objective. Because the artist himself enters into the process of creation with his whole mind and with all the force of his personality, he is able to draw meaning and content, its own deeper reality, out of the thing which he has encountered. To the inner image of this thing he responds in his own way, taking the worthwhile, which he finds there and rejecting the trivial; and the answer of Dürer to an encounter with violets will therefore be different from that of, say, Matisse. Thus the artist himself may undergo a catharsis through the inward process by which a work of art is realized. Paradoxically, from this standpoint we can understand how a cynical dissolute artist can sometimes surprise us with a work of astonishing purity and depth. He too may meet the moment of truth when through such an experience he sees himself, and pursues his inspiration.

The importance of the artist's initial response is very clear, for instance, in the poetry of the English Romantic Movement, or in Turner, or in the flower and animal painting of Pisanello. But the original impact may not come from the beauties of nature; it may be something which rouses the artist in all his senses, which can rage in the depth of his soul—one thinks of the poetry of love or of despair, of the sort of experience which enabled Shakespeare to write *King Lear* or Michelangelo to conceive his "Night". If faced with experience of this sort, the artist abandons himself to it, if he turns away from the personal and moral demands which it may make upon him, he will in the formulation of his work abandon also something of his own personality. On the other hand he may withstand the pull of intoxicating excitement, and disengage, out of deceptive illusions, a valid image, one which gives a clear and firm assent to a valid order. "There is music—one thinks of Bach and Beethoven—which curbs the most gigantic inner tension, which resolves the chaos of turbulence in a soul, and frees it into the cosmos of eternal law; here we see the evidence of the highest human determination and self-mastery, evidence both of facing up to this world, and acceptance of the values of the next. This is the artistic manifestation of human morality at its highest";[1] one can tell in a work of art whether at its birth the author has wrestled with an angel to win a blessing, or abandoned himself to demons.

Form in Art

Shattering internal experiences may come to very different kinds of people. The artist is distinguished from the rest by the fact that these experiences allow him no rest until he gives them some kind of expression, until he can find release from his inward tension through the creation of some corresponding sensible form. Form is the basis of all art. And in the last resort even the aesthetician has to accept it as a mystery. Here we are concerned with the moral aspect and will therefore merely attempt to exclude certain misunderstandings.

It is difficult for us to appreciate what form means to the artist. We may be burdened in advance by the scholastic notion of form as the abstract essence, or the structural principle of a particular thing—something invisible. Art cannot really be defined in these terms. The principle of art—beauty—is according to the scholastics *splendor formae*, the radiance of a "form" which can only be grasped intellectually. Alternatively it may be that we think of form too superficially, as something external, the product of calculation and technique.

Form in art is the child of "the inner-image", of manual skill, and of aesthetic gifts. Without the inspiring inner-image the artist is no more than a craftsman; without mastery of technique all that emerges is a more or less inspired piece of bungling; without aesthetic gifts there can be no identity between the artistic form and the inner-

---

[1] Wilhelm Waldstein, *Kunst und Ethos* (Salzburg, 1954).

image—that unity which both convinces and satisfies—
and without this there is no beauty.

If we are to understand what kitsch is it is important
not to misunderstand or narrowly interpret the idea of
beauty. Beauty is simply value in the sphere of art; it belongs to art as truth to science or good to ethics. It is not
therefore to be identified with harmony, which is the
principle of one sort of art only, the classical. As we have
seen, horror can also be given artistic form. Picasso's
Guernica is beautiful, in the sense of having artistic
value. Again the creative experience of the artist need
not be painful. Schubert may well have written some
of his greatest songs in a light-hearted mood in a
beer garden—the Elizabethans wrote exquisite lyrics in
taverns.

It is almost impossible to classify the great range of
means used by artists to give form to their inspiration.
There are all the different arts, poetry, music, painting,
etc., and within these the many different styles which have
evolved and developed. Then again the individual artist
varies in his approach; with some their work is often a
straightforward statement about an object as in, say, a
Chardin or a Dutch still-life, or it may evoke some deeper
reality, for example in Fra Angelico's paintings or those of
Rembrandt, or on a small scale Dürer's violets; or again it
may be the expression of personal feeling, as in Van Gogh's
passionate painting of turbulent cypresses or flaming sun-
flowers. The vast possibilities of difference in emotional
tension become apparent when one compares the dynamic
movement and terrifying sense of animal strength and
ferocity in Rubens' *Lion Hunt*, with the lyrical sophistica-
tions of Watteau's courtly scenes, or with Veit's *Rest on
the Flight into Egypt* (Plate 8). In this last, we are reaching
the frontiers of art. One is scarcely aware that it is com-

posed by a painter; were it not for the religious sincerity which speaks in the simplicity of the representation one might take it for a photograph. When painting does become photography, that is when it merely offers a reflection of the object painted, without any transformation of it through the mind of the artist, then it is no longer art. The camera, the tape-recorder, or in some cases the clearly formulated conceptual statement, can do this much better. Equally, however, the expression of vague feelings—as opposed to the imposition of artistic form on content—is also not art.

What determines the Value of a Work of Art?

We ask ourselves then, what is it that determines the value of a work of art? Firstly, it is the quality of the experience which is given artistic form, rather than the actual subject, which counts. Where quality is in some degree lacking, kitsch will slip in. A well-painted still life has greater value than an ill-painted Madonna both from tht aesthetic and from the religious point of view. When Dürer in his violets or his drawing of grasses reverently reproduces a small excerpt of creation as a whole, when Schubert in the *Winterreise* touchingly brings to life a human destiny, when Andrew Marvell praises his garden "annihilating all that's made to a green thought in a green shade"—those who have eyes to see or ears to hear are invited to share an experience of a reality which could not have been otherwise expressed; the sort of experience which is, as it were, open at either end, in the sense that thereby one finds oneself on the threshold of contemplation. These are experiences in fact which leave one far more disposed to prayer—sometimes indeed already caught up in prayer—than if one kneels before the sort of statue of our Lady which is to be found in most Catholic churches.

It follows that the extent to which a painting is faithful to the outward appearance of what is painted cannot be a criterion of the value of a work of art. Every work of art is both more and less than nature. Less because a painting is not real in the same sense as the object painted is real. Both less and more because every object, every bit of reality, can be a focal point for the most varied creative ideas, of which one artist will seize at the most upon two or three only. In painting a horse, for instance, one painter —such as Uccello—may be interested primarily in the formal beauty of its wonderful curves, a Leonardo may see it as the incarnation of strength and speed, whereas Stubbs will paint the individual animal observing all its particular points, and Delacroix will be aware of all sorts of romantic connotations which awake memories of the link between man and his steed. And so the work of art becomes also something more than nature—as we have already seen in discussing the creative process—and its value as a representation will depend not upon its photographic truth, but upon the impact which the artist's inner image makes upon the beholder, and the conviction which that carries.

Secondly, the value of a work of art is judged by its purely aesthetic, formal qualities—by the beauty and power and subtlety of the shapes created and organized therein. Discussion of these qualities is beyond the scope of this book, as kitsch never has its roots here.

Finally, there is an element which is not purely aesthetic but also moral; it is concerned with the artist as a human being and arises from the struggle which we have noted that he cannot avoid as the inner image of his subject grows within him and as he seeks to clarify it and finally

24

give it form. He cannot but meet this struggle with his human nature as a whole. We shall consider this in greater detail on page 32.

Art as Communication

All art is communication. Once an inner image has been made explicit in colour, in verse, or in melody, it has by this very fact acquired the character of a communication. Not in the sense of a mediation of knowledge—in this sense art is a very incomplete and circuitous communication—but with the idea of a sharing between the artist and those who look at or listen to his work. A sharing, a communication, in which both sides have to make a personal contribution; it is just this personal element which makes the "objective" evaluation of a work of art so difficult. We know from our own experience how the same song or picture can touch us deeply at one time and leave us quite cold at another. Or if our affections are engaged in regard to a particular artist, or if we are merely wanting to be clever, how much can be read into a work of art, or how much can be read out of it. The extent to which our judgment is liable to be affected by these subjective influences is one of the difficulties in the diagnosis of kitsch.

Our difficulties are further aggravated by the present state of society. When people belonged to a living, closed culture the content of experience was to a very large degree common, and so could be communicated in a language intelligible to all. Art in the sense of style was the expression not only of the individual artist but of the community. Both the form and the content of the expression of an individual experience—for instance, in a love song—represented also a common experience, easily understood and so easily shared by all.

25

What is Kitsch?

That is how it used to be. It was still so for Bach, but after Beethoven things began to change. The appreciation of art begins to be subjective, experienced in isolation, and also isolating in its effect. This process reached its apogee in the Romantic movement. It is true that since then we have been trying for a long time to find our way back to some more objective art, but we now lack the coherent common culture and there is no longer any art language which is universally understood. Hence it happens that artists, while striving for objectivity, actually make use of the most curious and subjective forms of expression, excogitated and often painfully laboured, very different from those which grow out of a living culture. This lack of an art language opens the door to kitsch, to an extent never before envisaged. This is one of the major difficulties which we face today.

There is, however, no need to resign ourselves to this situation. Technical progress, for instance, has led to the formation of an international form-language which extends out of the technical-utilitarian well into the artistic sphere. We see this in modern industrial architecture, in the design of modern forms of transport, furniture, domestic utensils, posters, etc. And even in their ideological isolation men are still human; when profound experience is linked with great artistic gift the language of art is widely intelligible, even today.

An analysis of art as communication can only sketch out the basis; it cannot detail the immense wealth of possibility. Two poles alone remain immovable; the artist must speak a personal language, and that language must be intelligible; somehow or other these two must be reconciled. In one direction even Beethoven approaches the limit in his last quartets when he makes use of a language so wilfully remote that many lovers of his *Fidelio*, his symphon-

26

ies, Masses and songs find it unintelligible. At the other end even a popular work of art, a song, say, expressing some commonplace human emotion simply and in familiar forms accessible to everyone, still cannot dispense with the unique, unexchangeable language of a particular and personal experience. This is so, for instance, in the case of folk songs which have become so much a part of the common heritage that even the name of the author is forgotten. Best-selling kitsch, however, also enters quickly, even more quickly, into the common heritage. The nearer we draw to the pole of intelligibility, the more we aim at general intelligibility, the nearer we are liable to come to kitsch.

The Response of the Beholder, Listener or Reader

We have considered the experience of the artist, but what of that of the beholder of his picture and the hearer of his music? Let us imagine someone standing before a work of art, knowing nothing of its creator and unaided by any interpreter. If, for instance, the work is a portrait he may recognize the sitter. If he sticks at this he gains factual knowledge, nothing more; but if after the first recognition he finds himself held, begins to feel that the man before him is looking at him, is in some solid way a living presence, then he is beginning to grasp the meaning of the portrait as a work of art. It has touched him personally.

There are things which may get in the way and prevent communication. In some people artistic sensibility is lacking, or undeveloped; even among intellectuals there are those who are notoriously backward in visual appreciation just as there are those who are tone deaf to music. They may even be able to recognize a style or artist but they do not respond to his message. Or again a person may be aesthetically sensitive but the experience evoked by the artist—as, for instance, religious ecstasy—may be something to which he has closed his mind, which has become inaccessible to him because he jumps to a Freudian interpretation perhaps, and so obstructs communication.

But if nothing intervenes, if, to return to a simple case, we think of Dürer's violets, or Mozart's melody, or Wordsworth's poem, what happens? We pay attention, we look or listen more closely, we are pleased. But that is not the end. We feel moved, we would like to be quiet and absorbed. What goes on in us is quite different from the noting of facts characteristic of scientific or practical thought; nor are we concerned with the considerations of the art expert, dates or attributions. Rather we find ourselves drawn into something inward, something vital, the inner-image which the artist has embodied in his work.

Is this really what happens? Or are we just interpreting our experience according to our ideas? By listening to a Beethoven *adagio* can we really find out what the artist meant? Looking at one of Kandinsky's abstract paintings can we with any degree of probability know the reality behind the inner image depicted? Hardly. Often we can be sure only that here is some basic human experience, some elemental emotion or condition of mind, a great excitement and opening outwards perhaps, or a sense of release, or of *lacrimae rerum*, the sadness of life. Though we cannot define what it says, art speaks to us. It not only touches us but it also works in us; it can be an experience which leaves us changed, conscious of new depths in our own souls.

We have just taken examples of abstract painting and absolute instrumental music; most works of art communicate in less ambiguous terms. Herein, however, may lie a danger; we may stop short at the subject—the thing which we recognize—it may overshadow and cut out that which the artist is communicating in and through it. We need sensibility to artistic form in order to be able to abandon ourselves, to open ourselves to its message; then delight in the work of art will bring insight into its deeper meaning and a sense of its symbolic function, then, contemplating Dürer's violets, we will find that suddenly, without knowing what has happened to us, we are aware of the meaning of silence, of truthfulness, of the lowliness of the creature.

The experience of a work of art is catalytic. Its effect is to deepen and purify our consciousness, to give confidence, bring peace, impart order. The artist through a personal commitment transforms the subject which is his starting-point, into an inner image which he communicates to us in his work. He communicates and shares with us. Art is an instance of the mystery of human interdependence, of the fact that it is only through encounters with others, through meetings in an "I-thou", that is a personal, as it were naked, relationship, that we are able to be really alive. When we experience a work of art as the message of its maker, when we share in his inner intimate world, the nature of things is more readily unfolded to us and we savour where hitherto we had merely observed. In a thousand ways in everyday life we have the same experience as the fledgling whose food is first chewed for it by its mother. Where reality is mirrored for us in the experience of our fellow-men, more especially in the grace-given, intensive, and rich experience of our brother the artist, it strikes us more forcefully, and becomes more fruitful in us. Because of his gifts and his moments of inspiration and creation, his experience is greater than ours. For those who can respond he is always, like a parent, someone greater.

What is Kitsch?

What touches us first in a work of art is the magic of its form, then within this form we find the life of another person intimately communicated to us, and so enriching us.

II

Art and Morality

The Artist and Morality

We have seen that both the creation and the appreciation of art involve the whole man. Aesthetics, therefore, must involve moral considerations. The more clearly we see the relationship the better shall we understand about kitsch.

Should the artist aim at edification in his work? If we remove pietistic overtones from the word, we can say that at the least the artist may legitimately wish to do so. It is an intention that he can have in mind, but it cannot enter into the process of creation; here what he does must be done for its own sake, directed by artistic considerations alone. The artist is neither a moralist nor a pedagogue. While he is working he cannot be casting side-glances at the educational effect of his work. He can, of course, before beginning a work offer all his effort to God and in doing so imprint upon it a whole way of life given to God in conformity with the moral order. But this must not prevent him from becoming completely involved in receiving and responding to the demands of his art as such. The act of creation springs from a spontaneous reaction, a sort of ecstasy of love for its initial inspiration and the form which it takes must be the concentrated expression of an inner reaction; in other words, it is a statement of values, uninfluenced by outside considerations. Is this not dangerous? So is everything worth doing. Only by burying our talents can we avoid danger, and he who does so is judged already.

Morality comes in because the artist is involved in his work as a whole man; and the point at which morality comes in is right at the beginning, with the first impression of the thing which motivates his impulse to create. That it is this particular thing rather than another which moves him and determines his line of approach, will depend upon his *ordo amoris*, on what holds value for him in general. Our attention is drawn most easily to that in which our own feelings are involved; the moral quality of the artist works as a filter, clarifying or obscuring his perception of reality. When prudence enables him to adapt himself realistically, and when the other cardinal virtues assist him to be prudent, then a man of moral integrity—given adequate talent—will at the very first contact be attracted to what is important and essential. Unlike the pleasure-seeker who sees in reality, or in place of reality, solely that which promises enjoyment, he will be able to see and feel things as they are. Associations play an important part— the fragrance of a violet might well remind a St Francis de Sales of the fragrance of the spiritual, *Christi bonus odor*, while to a womanizer it recalls hours of scented dalliance. Where one artist may react to his impulse with a burst of passion, to be mastered only with effort, before he can weigh the nature and value of its cause, another may be able to respond with the docility and sensitivity of an open mind.

It is from this standpoint that we should understand Pius XII's requirement that sacred art should be undertaken only by artists who are religious and morally serious: "So the artist who has no religious faith or whose thoughts and way of life are far removed from God, ought not on any account to put his hand to religious art. His soul lacks the power of seeing what God's majesty demands, what his worship requires. Works of art that have no religious inspiration may perhaps proclaim an artist of experience and of some technical ability. But they cannot express religion and faith in a way becoming to God's house and its holiness."[2]

It is not inconsistent with this statement to say that it is possible for an artist who belongs to no Church, or even for a non-Christian artist, to make a work of art that is both religious and Christian;[3] what is necessary, apart from adequate factual knowledge, is that he should have a religious attitude, that he should work with a consciousness of the holy and divine. Indeed, as we have already noted, even an artist of immoral life can through a moment of longing for his better self produce genuine religious art.

It thus becomes clear that it is not so much in the subject as in the artist's treatment of it that morality comes into art. Morally indifferent, even evil subjects can provide material for art. For instance, Fellini's film *La Strada* created an atmosphere in which God and moral laws did not appear to exist—it is about a South Italian girl, sold by her mother to be the mistress and assistant of a travelling mountebank—nevertheless its treatment, the awakening of selfless love in the girl, the intimation that even this bleak social milieu is open to a higher reality, made itself felt so strongly that one came away uplifted rather than depressed. On the other hand the well-meant, edifying "happy ending" is often kitsch because it attempts to portray the world as more comfortable and comforting than it really is. Indeed the representation of evil in art is not merely permissible, it is necessary material; but it must be

---

[2] Encyclical *Musicae sacrae disciplina* (1955).
[3] For instance, the Stations of the Cross at Leyland, Lancashire, by Dooley, a non-Christian.

treated in the light of the moral order, and an artist can do this only when he himself—at least temporarily—accepts this order.

Moral qualities are therefore involved in the elaboration of the artist's experience, as well as at the time of his initial response. As human beings we do not see with immediate clarity the whole significance of the casual encounter; effort is necessary, listlessness and sloth, all kinds of confused feelings and desires, have to be overcome before the inner image is achieved.

Again, the artist may unravel his experience too superficially, either with too cold and pedantic an approach, or with too uncontrolled a zest; or he may be exposed to the demonic power of archetypes, abandoning his need to discipline primitive images and urges. Finally, there may be a personal failure. An artist may be aware of and disturbed by a sense of the good and the holy, but he may refuse to respond or may make use of his sensibility as a means for selfish ends—in some pictures one can see that art has been used as a means of bread-winning, or indeed of making as much money as possible.

Again, an artist endowed with great natural gifts may be so fascinated by the forms which come to him so easily that he is tempted to let them become as it were self-sufficient, to play with them so that his work becomes a mere aesthetic exercise and so loses any existential quality or personal seriousness. One can distinguish, even in the work of great artists, between a frivolous sketch and a work, maybe only a pencil drawing, where the artist has put his heart into every line. Or again the senses—since it is with these that the artist is concerned in giving form to his image—may be roused so that they threaten the purity of his work. For instance, when painting a picture of our Lady, the artist may have responded with reverence to his

34

inner image, but in the process of giving it visual form his idea of the mother of God may take on the traits of an imaginary partner of earthly love. This is particularly likely to occur during periods when the contemporary artistic vocabulary makes a powerful appeal to the senses, raising difficulties for Wagner which did not exist for Bach, for Venetian painters of the Renaissance which were unknown to the Siennese.

It is important to note that all these types of moral failure are integral to the artist's activity as an artist, they enter into the actual process of creation, influence the evolution of the artistic form of the work produced, and are perceptible in this. But we cannot pretend that, in our mis-shaped, ordinary world, artistic and moral values completely coincide; to maintain as much would be to betray unrealistic moralism or an equally remote optimistic aestheticism. A work of art of very great worth may still betray personal and moral immaturity, just as indeed whole periods in the history of art, in spite of inspired achievements, also reveal disturbing deficiencies in their image of man. Wagner's orchestral compositions, despite their great musical attainment, often betray a blatant sensuality, and so fail to reach the greatest spiritual heights. On the other hand a touchingly sincere, morally irreproachable approach can be associated with so little intensity of personal experience or with such feeble powers of expression that the work produced will gain our respect for the good will behind it, but fail to move or impress us.

The fact that the artistic process, the imposition of form, involves moral qualities, and that the experience represented is as important as the forms by which it is represented, means that the doctrine of art for art's sake must be repudiated. Obedience to the internal laws of form alone is not enough. This doctrine involves a loss of essential life; form can no more be independent of content than the body can remain alive without the soul.

Morality and the Beholder

In the presence of a statue of Christ a person may make an act of faith and charity. This act is morally good, but it is in the first place a response, not to the work of art itself, but to its subject.

One can approach a work of art with the attitude: does it edify me? does it help me in my religious life? But to do so is to put a barrier between oneself and the artist, to impede what he is trying to communicate in the language of art. And this is ultimately impeding what God himself is trying to communicate to us; for God gave this language to man, and God does nothing in vain.

We need, then, to allow a work of art to speak to us in its own way, and so we should suppress all preconceptions of what it should or should not do. In this way we can share the God-given experience of the artist, an encounter that can enrich our whole life. The beholder, like the artist, has to respond unreservedly with his whole being. He also, therefore, is morally involved. Herein lies the real edification of art.

But as with the artist, in practice aesthetic and moral enrichment do not always coincide. Sometimes the viewer may inwardly go beyond what the artist offers; for instance, he may by-pass the suggestions of sentimentality and frivolity which may be inherent in the painter's style, to concentrate ultimately on the true aesthetic quality of the work, say the representation of a saint, and so respond to the artist's essential vision more sincerely and profoundly than the artist himself—and one thinks of a possible approach to rococo statues, or to the religious prints of a mannerist artist such as Bellange.

On the other hand the viewer or hearer often fails to respond with adequate perception or depth to the artist's communication. We have already seen how he may respond only to formal values, turning away from the deeper meaning which they convey. Someone, for instance, who listens to a Mozart *Agnus Dei* as if it were merely a part of a concert may receive only a very superficial impression.

To joy in art God has attached labour and effort, and this includes moral effort. And this is especially true in regard to religious art; because here the subject is something of intrinsic value, and there is always a tendency to respond to that alone, and to consider the artistic values by which it is mediated as "distracting". But in this case we might as well dispense with the work of art altogether and take the religious idea direct from a prayer-book or textbook. In so doing we should, however, lose not only aesthetic pleasure but a more profound and pure experience than our own of precisely this religious subject.

From the beholder art demands not only sensibility and training but humility and responsiveness. These are related to the moral qualities of readiness and maturity; in return the artistic experience will enrich us morally as well as aesthetically.

III

The Origins of Kitsch

With the Artist

THE purpose of our outline in the last chapter of the theory of aesthetic experience and its relation to ethics was to enable us to see at which precise point kitsch is liable to insinuate itself into art. If the decisive factors in a work of art are the artist's aesthetic gifts, his inner-image, and his manual dexterity, then the main root of kitsch seems to lie in the second of these: when an artist's experience is trashy, the work which he produces is likely to be kitsch—aesthetic trash. There are two prior possibilities to be considered however, before we analyse this complex idea.

What about aesthetic ability? Can it be that when this is deficient kitsch creeps in? We all know many examples of religious painting and sculpture in progressive modern churches, or products of the German Nazarene school or of followers of the Pre-Raphaelites, which are transparently and genuinely religious in intention, but where the creative experience of the artist is too weak, so that the composition lacks conviction, the utterance is feeble. What is lacking here is artistic value, beauty in the full sense of the word; also a failure to transcend the incoherence of the age and the loss of a common symbolic language—already noted. But kitsch is present only when what is artistically inadequate is also insipid or repulsive. Indeed, we may tend to reject as kitsch (if only because they are mass-produced) some devotional objects which do not deserve the condemnation; we feel that they lack spirit, life, artistic worth; or that the manufacturers have not properly grasped the idea of what they wanted to produce. These inadequacies do not make kitsch. It is not therefore ability or lack of ability which differentiates that which is kitsch from that which is not kitsch.

Again, may not the element of kitsch be present from the very beginning in the subject which is the artist's starting-point? We all know the road lined with birch-trees against a background of heather in bloom under a blue heaven and a few white clouds; or the sunset where orange melts into rose, where the landscape is aetherialized and romanticized in the last rays of departing light. When one analyses one's reaction to such scenes, one realizes that nature seems kitsch because we are equating it with memories of numberless sentimental pictures, of some over-coloured reproductions, or of naturalistic paintings designed for cheap effect—the kitsch in fact is not in nature, but in our own minds.

The way in which an artist—or the viewer—chooses to see his subject may therefore lead almost irresistibly to kitsch. Here, then, at the very first moment of contact between the artist's mind and his subject the possibility of kitsch really begins. We can best analyse it through particular examples.

Plate 3 is entitled *The Infant Jesus with St John and two Angels*. It is immediately obvious that the painting has little to do with either Jesus or the Baptist; anyone looking at it without prejudice might take it to be just a charming painting of cherubs. Kitsch? Of course not. The discrepancy is between the picture and its designation, not in the picture itself; one can think of many paintings of a mother and child labelled *Madonna and Child*, where there is a similar lack of religious intention. We can wonder perhaps at the mentality which put a religious title to a secular picture, but there is no question of kitsch.

We turn to two very different examples where the kitsch does seem to lie in the subject. Plates 4 and 5 reproduce two "holy pictures" which obviously do not correspond to the themes chosen by the artist. Plate 4 purports to portray the Eucharistic Christ present in the tabernacle. As a representation of the Redeemer offered in sacrifice and crucified, we are offered a little fellow with a curly head archly peeping from behind the tabernacle curtain. He appeals naturally enough to the heart of the normal woman or child. But is this the way which we ought to be touched by the love of God made man, a love enduring to the terrible end of the Cross, which the Eucharistic species should call to mind? As soon as we raise this question we cease to be charmed and begin to be shocked and horrified. It is disgraceful to try to awaken a religious response so easily on such a superficial, emotional plane. Kitsch here consists in the disingenuous choice of subject together with the aim of gaining a cheap effect. Plate 4 comes from Germany; Plate 5 is sold in London. The latter is one of a set of cards purposing to give a visual expression to the gifts of the Holy Spirit. Again we have a great theological doctrine reduced to the trivial and cosy; in itself the picture is pretty in a senti-mental way, and it evokes a corresponding response. The gift of the Fear of the Lord is reduced to something like pink icing on a birthday cake.

Of very different scale and pretension is Plate 6 which reproduces a very popular painting, Salvador Dali's *Christ of St John of the Cross*. Our Lord is represented as a young man with beautiful curly hair. His body is painted very realistically but without any signs of the suffering of the

Passion. The Cross is dramatically lit by a strong cross light, but the striking thing about the picture is the angle of view, the beholder looking down upon Christ. It may be that devout people glancing at the picture can pass on to a meditation on our Lord's contemplation of succeeding generations of men from the Cross. Studying the picture, however, one becomes aware that the viewpoint is a trick to catch attention, while in itself it is fundamentally unsuitable that we should look down on the Cross, just as the idea of a trick painting of the crucifixion is fundamentally blasphemous, as is the realism used to make our Lord physically attractive. There is no inkling either of the divinity, or of the redemptive sacrifice of Christ. The same artist's painting of the *Sacrament of the Last Supper* (Plate 7), in Washington, is again an attempt to arouse religious devotion in a cheap way; two apostles kneel in the foreground, dressed in magnificent white silk cloaks, their heads devoutly bent, like romantic actors playing a part, not like simple men at an overwhelming moment. The partial nakedness of the Christ figure is again painted with great realism, emphasized by the fade-away torso above, which is like some cheap cinema effect; the whole effect indeed is like a painting of a still from some film of the life of Christ. The artist, in fact, has not been concerned with what really happened, either in its historic simplicity, or in its theological momentousness, but with the effect which he can make out of it and engender in the mind of the beholder.

These three examples are very diverse in scale, subject and artistic talent; they all, however, illustrate the point that when a religious theme is selected and treated according to the artist's fancy, when it is subjected to a first arbitrary conception which does not correspond with reality, then there is kitsch; a trashy experience is already involved. This becomes much more obviously the cause of kitsch when we consider this arising at that point in the evolution of a work of art which we have called the "inner image".

Here, too, we must be cautious. Not every defect leads to kitsch. Plate 8 reproduces *Rest on the Flight into Egypt* by Philip Veit, a painter of the German Nazarene school. This is a sincere religious picture—certainly not kitsch. The artist's inner image has grown out of meditation on his subject and the work breathes an atmosphere of deep peace and religious feeling. We can believe that this Madonna is really using this moment of rest to enter more deeply into the mystery of her child. Nevertheless, the picture does not touch us at the deepest level. It is too peaceful, too facile in its piety. It is clear that in the mind of the artist the scene has been transformed into an inner-image in which certain values have been emphasized and isolated and others played down so as to create an artificial harmony. These people are not hunted refugees in a barren desert but are enjoying idyllic peace in an Arcadian landscape. Reality has first been smoothed out and only then given artistic expression. A picture of this kind, by avoiding all disturbing facts and jarring notes, creates a gentle, placid atmosphere in which there is an element of complacency which can very rapidly become a means of cheap stimulation leading to unmistakable kitsch. We maintained at the beginning that this painting is not kitsch. We can now be more precise: it is not yet kitsch.

If we go one step further we are in the undoubted realm of kitsch. Plate 9 shows us *Mary as the Good Shepherdess*. One may well begin by raising a theological query in regard to the subject; is it permissible to apply to Mary the title of the Good Shepherd, he who gives his life for his sheep, a title which Christ applied to himself to bring out the very pith of his mission as Saviour? Even leaving this aside, what sort of impression does the picture make on us? How does it differ from the Nazarene painting? The whole thing strikes one as bogus. It is not merely the permutation of sex roles which seems artificial and unreal. Here the colouring is flat, the drawing weak, and Mary's face is notably emptier, with a conventional sweetness. The sheep are obviously well-behaved and affectionate, and the "ideal" landscape is remote from the possibility of storms or "ravening wolves". What need of a shepherdess in such conditions? Is this the world into which Christians are sent as sheep among wolves? Is this Mary who provided for the child Jesus with the work of her hands, and who held to the *fiat* uttered in the angel's presence right up to the foot of the Cross? In such a world Mary no longer appears as the refuge of sinners, comforter of the unhappy, queen among martyrs: that has all been glossed over, here the safe and harmless Christian soul is already in paradise (albeit a somewhat boring one).

Possibly there is in this picture some sincere religious intention, though little artistic gift or inspiration. It is a question of honest kitsch, unaware of its worthlessness, but still kitsch. That element in the subject which seemed desirable to the artist has been dreamed out of its context, out of its contact with reality, in such a way that its untruthfulness immediately imposes itself upon the mind of the viewer; it is characteristic of this spuriousness that a very cheap way of creating the desired mood is used. A picture gives a false view of reality—and therefore of religion—it is incapable of comforting anyone in real need and provides no resources for achieving the Christian life.

In England, Sir Joshua Reynolds' painting of *The Infant Samuel* (Plate 10) is a very popular religious picture. It is in a different category from the modern German drawing,

Plate 4. The subject is neither so sublime, nor is there cheapness here in its treatment, nor formal artistic qualities. This is not kitsch. All the same it is not a very adequate representation of the terrifying message given to Samuel, nor does it give one any inkling of the strong and ruthless man he was to become. Its popularity, one imagines, arises from the representation it offers of the innocence of childish prayer. And this perhaps was Reynolds' intention in accordance with his classical aesthetic theories, of painting the ideal rather than the particular; but as such it is the precursor of countless images of baby angels and chubby representations of "baby Jesus", such as Plate 11, where the intention is not to give form to any ideal, but to make a cheap appeal. Here our Lord is reduced to a childish figure with a disproportionate head and features, in a nightgown (why a nightgown?), and the children whom he addresses are drawn according to the same formula. The relationship between them is merely sentimental. As a representation to be given to a child it is trashy in conception, and cheap and slovenly in execution. In so far as it is liked by adults—who after all are the people who buy this "twee" religious art—it seems to denote infantilism in their religious life. The untruthfulness of the image is patent: God became a child for us, the artist has turned him into a cuddly doll.

There is kitsch here in the subject, the inner-image and the form—from start to finish.

Let us now turn to *The Penitent Magdalene* (Plate 13). The subject is traditional, it shows the saint in the legendary setting of a cave with a pious book and a skull in front of her. But what has this become in the imagination, and afterwards in the representation of the artist? The subject has been given a meaning which does not correspond to its reality. Not only is it far removed from the idea of a fasting penitent mortifying the flesh, but there is in fact nothing which corresponds to the New Testament figure of the woman to whom much was forgiven because she loved much. This woman with half-bared breast, loose golden hair, careless posture is an erotic attraction arousing sexual desire.

The painter of this picture was an artist. On the formal plane there is no cheapness; nor would there necessarily be cheapness in the expression of eroticism, were that on the level of basic human experience; what makes this kitsch is the fact that a titillation of the senses is brought in under cover of piety. This is evil kitsch; for the naïve viewer it is scandal in the biblical sense.

The nature of kitsch is particularly easy to see in this form. It is worthwhile therefore to bring out how an artist may come to produce it in order to make money. He knows that most people are particularly responsive to sensual-erotic stimulation and that many are inhibited from admitting this either to themselves or to others. He has, therefore, to produce something which provides a legitimate cover for its erotic interest. So he chooses a suitable biblical or saintly figure, indicating her identity by sacred symbols which disarm moral criticism, and carefully avoiding suggestions of her actual life or real personality.

In a true work of art the world of sense, and pleasure through the senses, is seized upon and mastered by higher values. In this process they lose that self-sufficiency which tends towards mere sensual pleasure, and become instead the vehicle for a spiritual content; external beauty is intensified by embodying a beauty of the spirit. Evil kitsch exhibits the opposite process; higher values are used and dragged down to sensual—undesirable—ends and so poisoned. In this spuriousness and hypocrisy lies the element of kitsch.

What is Kitsch?

One way to make the desired impression is by formal means—ones which are easily grasped, such as glossy textures and bright colours, or simple harmonies and easy rhythms in music. Anything requiring effort from viewer or hearer is avoided. So the saint is never an individual, but a type of the "sweet woman", a puppet, really a mere neuter, an erotic doll.

The Magdalene picture may be more common to German than in English or American homes, but Plate 12 shows a picture of similar intention—though without artistic value this time—which is a post-war product manufactured for a very wide market. The girl is dressed and posed in a way which immediately shows that she is meant to represent our Lady, but her face is that of a film-star or pin-up girl. It is the dressing up, the exploitation of religious associations, and the consequent hypocrisy which makes this kitsch. If a sense experience and nothing else were involved then there would be no question of kitsch, or of art.

We have considered how kitsch can enter at the point where the artist first evolves his inner image, comparing kitsch examples with those not yet kitsch. Finally let us see whether kitsch can enter at the formal aesthetic level. Kitsch will of course appear in the form of an artist's work if it has already entered into his inner experience. When the artist's experience is trashy even great aesthetic gifts and extraordinary ability will not prevent him from producing kitsch. Even Holbein in some of his religious paintings showed an entirely superficial sense of the spiritual, and Carlo Dolci and Guido Reni have provided some of the most popular sentimental religious art; Salvador Dali, as we have seen, paints kitsch, though there is no question of his great talent and skill.

The artist may also be consciously unfaithful to a real

inner experience and slovenly in giving form to it. This does not necessarily lead to kitsch unless the artist lapses into false conventional forms, or does not bother to work out his forms at all, allowing them to be dictated by his pen or brush—as easily happens in modernistic or abstract kitsch. It is here that the dilemma of the modern world, the lack of a common artistic language, and in particular of a common language of religious symbolism, has opened wide the door to kitsch.

Let us again take a concrete example to illustrate our meaning. Plate 14 is an English counterpart of the Nazarene school, a Pre-Raphaelite picture, Holman Hunt's well-known painting *The Light of the World*. This is certainly not kitsch : Holman Hunt was a painter who was deeply religious, a gifted artist of great integrity who took infinite pains to try to create his representations of Christian themes in terms of the real world around him. This painting was made just before his journey to the Holy Land, an ambition from childhood, undertaken in order to "use my powers to make more tangible Jesus Christ's history and teaching". Yet there is something wrong with this picture. It lies surely in the fact that while Hunt's thought was symbolic, his terms are those of extreme realism. The artist has himself described his idea in words. Christ is dressed as king and priest, he stands knocking on the door of the obstinately closed mind, cumbered by the weeds of neglect and sloth, he comes with the lamp of the Word, "for the night is far spent and day is at hand". This is pure symbolism but it is exterior to the form, and therefore not explicit in it. The weeds are just weeds, not sins; our Lord is painted as a man, carefully studied and precise in every detail, yet the artist did not mean to suggest that he ever knocked on such a door, or wore such clothes. There is a hiatus between the artist's thought and the

47

form in which he is able to express it which in an earlier period would have been bridged by a normal familiarity with symbolism in the mind of the viewer. It was only in *The Scapegoat*, where the representation itself is symbolic, that Hunt succeeded in creating a really moving religious picture.

The Light of the World is not kitsch, but it created and popularized, with the help of many other remembered pictures, an image which is kitsch. Plate 15 shows a typical Sacred Heart card. Here the incompatibility of realism and symbolism is explicit; the representation of a realistic heart on top of our Lord's clothes is immediately repugnant. The repugnancy is only glossed over by the sloppiness of the realism. Hunt's carefully studied Jewish priestly robe has become a fancy-dress cloak and nightgown, Christ's face a sort of identikit compilation from old master "types". The sincerity and scrupulous effort which redeems Hunt's work has been replaced by commercialism and shoddy reproduction, with a veneer of sentimentality. In what way does this sloppy figure convey any idea of God-made-man and his burning, demanding love?

One can see that there has been no attempt at a transformation of the subject in the artist's mind. In such cases a representation is dashed off in a form easy to understand, known to suit public taste, formulated with calculated slovenliness. Here, where the aim is to make a quick profit and the artist is prepared to prostitute his gifts, there will frequently, indeed nearly always, be present what we have now discovered to be the recurrent distinguishing marks of kitsch: untruthfulness and brazen inferiority in representation. A great deal of commercial kitsch comes into existence in this way.

Plate 16 shows three examples of kitsch in "holy" pictures, chosen at random. How can we describe them? The first (16a) is apparently the child Jesus (or is it Mary as a child?) in a setting of spring blossoms, making twigs into the form of a cross. It is certainly the expression of a trashy experience. The second (16b) represents a saint (or is it the boy Christ?), with a stereotyped face and an expression of near imbecility; at the bottom a weightless cross has been introduced without relevance, presumably for the sake of trade, if not even with a concealed sneer. In 16c there is an even stronger impression of shamelessness. The tint is lilac, and each item in the whole artificial concoction, the drawing of the nose and eyes, the sloppy delineation of the dress, the careless placing of the crown of thorns, the meaningless doves (or are they symbols of souls nourished by the Eucharist?), their picking at the ears of wheat (actually barley), the commonplace expression of the face—everything in fact about the picture is repulsive. Anyone with any genuine religious experience would have been incapable of producing such a thing. It is simply a question of business with limited pious liability.

Of course trash in the form cannot be completely separated from trash in the experience. The barely concealed cynicism of this last example may be rare, but where the form is not only careless but trashy, it may be deduced that the artist's inner experience is likely also to be cheap and trivial.

Kitsch enters into form very easily in our time because it is aided by the machine. A work of art is by its nature a symbol of man: a man is alive only when nothing intervenes between his soul and body—such intervention in fact means death. Similarly in a work of art its creator's experience has to find direct expression in every detail—every note, every brush-stroke of his work. As soon as a third element, mechanical reproduction, whether in the form of reproductive printing, or of record or radio transmission, comes between the creative experience of the artist and that which is actually seen or heard, then this totality and immediacy is lost. The mechanical comes in between like a veil, or even a curtain, the turbulent, primitive force of the experience no longer speaks for itself. If it is perceived only through this veil there is a much greater danger of the beholder or the listener failing to experience and to respond to its proper meaning, and of misusing it as a means to other ends. And so kitsch finds an easier entry both into aesthetic expression and aesthetic response.

In addition there are defects inherent in technical reproduction. For instance, a colour-print seldom renders fine transitions; it simplifies (or distorts) colours and thus predisposes the viewer to a cheapened experience. If we compare, say, an original Raphael with even the best reproduction (and the reproductions sold in Catholic repositories are often of the crudest quality), the latter will in effect be nearer to kitsch than the original.

Finally, mere multiplication makes for kitsch. No matter how personal and immediate the feeling poured, say, by Botticelli, into his painting of the Madonna, as soon as this unique figure gazes at us from a dozen shop windows, it becomes a type, something available in quantity and therefore impersonal. Thence it is an easy step to make use of it for some other purpose, and so to move in the direction of kitsch.

The Origin of Kitsch in the Viewer

Art is by its nature intended to be a communication. The viewer—or listener—must participate. He may, however, be unable or unwilling to understand the artistic language of the work before him. It may be that he lacks aesthetic appreciation, or that, for the moment, he does not approach the particular work with an open mind and full attention: so it leaves him cold. There may, however, be another possibility; he may have an experience which is apparently aesthetic but which is in fact kitsch. In practice this is, for most of us, the real danger. The creative producers of kitsch are few, but no one is free from the liability to slip into kitsch in his enjoyment of a picture or a song. Our analysis of the origins of kitsch from the point of view of the artist is relevant to the understanding of kitsch in the reaction of the viewer, but it is also useful to consider this by itself.

First of all let us limit the field of enquiry. Not every pseudo-artistic experience is kitsch. Suppose someone has spent a lot of money on an abstract painting. He stands now in front of his picture and is pleased with it. Why? It may well be that it is not the picture itself but the price which he paid for it which inspires his pleasure.

Or again, a devout soul may look through the pages of a prayer book, find a picture of the Little Flower, St Thérèse of Lisieux, and be delighted with it. Is this an artistic experience? The person in question may think that she is taking pleasure in a beautiful picture: in fact the sight of her favourite saint has such a power of suggestion that though it arouses what seems to be artistic response, she is actually completely unaware of the message of the picture—artistic or otherwise.

When it is really a question of kitsch, as we have seen, this is not necessarily inherent in the work of art. Even a great work of art may be experienced as kitsch. This is particularly easy where the subject of the work is one which is open to such an interpretation—for instance, the death of a girl-saint, or indeed many pictures of the Passion, particularly when reproduction veils the personal touch of the painter. Or again perhaps, the artist's inner-image does not inform its expression with sufficient power, so that the beholder is apt to be too much involved in the superficial attraction of the work, and what it represents, without seeking behind this for its real content. Even a genuine aesthetic experience may turn into kitsch. When we have once been touched by the joy of a genuine work of art it is natural to want to repeat the experience; our joy came about because we were wholly absorbed in the work of art, gripped both by its form and its inner content, completely self-forgetful. Such an experience costs strength and effort and so does its renewal; it is much easier merely to renew the joy of recollecting the experience; even when actually looking at the picture, our contact with the work itself becomes merely superficial. While at the beginning a genuine aesthetic joy was present, now we are using the work of art for mere gratification—which is kitsch.

Finally we come to cases in which the work itself is definitely kitsch. Let us take a hymn such as *Immaculate Mary our hearts are on fire* which is kitsch in itself. What happens when this is also experienced as kitsch? We need to distinguish between several planes of such experience.

First of all it may be a simple, innocuous form of kitsch enjoyment. We want to sing and to pray as we sing. The hymn provides a cheap and pleasurable way of doing this; we enjoy it, though that is not the reason why we sing. At the same time mind and heart are not involved, or at most they provide a little background piety. There is no entering into the hymn as a real prayer, no personal speaking to Mary. We think we are taking part in a religious act when actually we are merely finding a pleasant sense experience in the harmony of the melody and the easily accessible emotional text with its smooth religious imagery. If there is a sin in this half-experience it is one of sloth, a failure to respond to the religious subject.

A lower plane is reached when the hymn—which should be sung-prayer—is just the occasion for a sloppy, ready-made enjoyment of melody, of major and minor, and drearily sweet religious image, and thought, patterns. The hymn is sung consciously in a sentimental way and for the singer's own immediate satisfaction regardless of the person to whom it is addressed—the Mother of God.

The danger of becoming involved in kitsch is naturally greatest when the object itself is kitsch; in some cases it is so obtrusive that we are immediately repelled as in the pictures on Plate 16, or hymns such as the one we have just instanced. But we must not deceive ourselves; even someone who is by no means insensitive to kitsch does not always recognize it at first sight, only afterwards he becomes aware that he has been taken in by it: nor indeed is the border line between kitsch and art easily distinguished. Kitsch is for every one of us a constant and not easily perceptible danger.

What then is Kitsch?

As the result of our analysis it is possible to propose two decisive factors which must always be present, and present together if we are to speak of kitsch: the bogus, spurious, untruthful (*Unechtheit*), and cheapness. The spurious or untruthful element is comparatively easy to identify, one recognizes that the true nature, importance and intrinsic value of the chosen theme are either not understood or not made manifest; instead we are offered its superficial aspect only, that is in so far as another more utilitarian meaning has not been substituted for the supposed theme. In brief, a claim is made for a work of art or an experience, that it is serious, when no serious effort has been involved.

What is Kitsch?

Untruthfulness alone does not, however, necessarily create kitsch. A forgery, for instance, is deception without kitsch. Kitsch results only when the impulse of cheapness, inferiority, inadequacy to the subject, is associated with the spuriousness. It is difficult to define this more precisely, but perhaps it may be made clearer by a series of juxtapositions. We may say that when kitsch is present either in a work of art, or in the response to a work of art, it is then a question not of something which has intrinsic value, but of something with immediate appeal to the viewer: not of something real in itself, won with arduous effort, but of something superficial, usually appealing merely to the senses, and lacking any symbolic life, because the form does not embody any value content: not of something personal and unique, but of the comfortable cliché and the easiest formula to hand; not of a response on the part of the viewer to the significance of the artist's creation, but of a short-cut made without regard or respect for the former—a short-cut probably aimed simply at the maximum gratification for the minimum effort, but which can also be aimed at using the work for ulterior, inferior ends—for instance, for the sensation of religious uplift: not of giving a true form to the inner-image but of dexterous hands or a fluent tongue finding a quick way to get an effect—using therefore blatant, crude and noisy means of expression.

If we combine all this with the idea of spuriousness, we arrive at the definition: kitsch is a work or experience within the field of art which is inadequate because it is bogus and cheap.

IV

Kitsch and the World Today

Sentimentality

THERE is no doubt that sentimentality runs riot in the realm of kitsch. Nevertheless kitsch and sentimentality are not the same thing.

Not all kitsch is sentimental; sometimes it is so inept and insipid that it does not even express anything as positive as sentimentality. And again, there is kitsch which is not sentimental, but rational, which titillates reason instead of sense and feeling: it can be called allegorical, a sort of bogus symbolic art where there is no real connection between the idea and the form. This has already come up in our discussion of Plate 15, where however the sentimental cannot be said to be lacking; its complement is the "modern" picture where the artist has recognized the possibilities of symbolism and exploited them cheaply.

Nor is everything sentimental kitsch. There are experiences which are internal only, without visible expression; or the outward form may make no claim to artistic status (as so easily happens in the case of that sentimentality which is disastrous to moral and religious life).

Kitsch and sentimentality are nevertheless so closely linked that it is important to examine the idea of sentimentality, particularly in our age, which, despite appearances to the contrary, is particularly liable to its seductions. We live in a rationalist period. To a degree hitherto unknown the powers of nature have been exploited, tamed, and brought into man's service. These achievements have demanded the interest, the vitality and the strength of whole generations. We no longer have much time for leisure and little sympathy for an attitude to life which is capable, or willing, to contemplate depths of human feeling.

Nor is feeling as such highly valued. It is less precise than philosophical or technical thinking, less clear-cut than a deliberate decision of the will. Moreover, it seems much more closely involved in our physical life than either thinking or willing. What a man feels is much more apparent than what he thinks. And finally the normal person is at least potentially master of his will and his thoughts, but not of his feelings.

All this may at any time be nullified by a new romanticism, but we must not forget that the whole of Western thought since the classical age of Greek philosophy has been constantly influenced by dualistic tendencies, openly or tacitly depreciating non-rational factors. Is it surprising then that modern man does not want publicly to attach much importance to feeling, or—worse—that he unconsciously represses it? And yet fine feeling is as valuable as clear thinking, it reveals to us the depths of the human spirit, its heart, and makes us aware of realities which the reason cannot grasp, or of which it would otherwise be ignorant.

The powers and resources which our souls possess, and which God has given us for a purpose, can only apparently be ignored or suppressed. Since Freud we know how much can proliferate below the surface, unrecognized and therefore uncontrolled and sub-human. When a person has not accepted his emotional life, he must reckon with the fact that his feelings will pass through him—willing steeds in the hands of that anonymous power which theologians describe as concupiscence, the result of original sin.

It is at the point where modern man relaxes, lets himself go, that it becomes apparent how far his feelings are corrupted and decayed. Listen to an old folk-song with its wealth of feeling—merry or austere—and then switch on the radio and let the pop songs rain down. Here where it is a question only of entertainment, not of working and making money, the modern man is ready to abandon himself to feeling, and we can see what is growing under the surface, under the cover of our rationalized daily life. Precisely those forms of experience which can give immediate and personal expression to the stirrings of man's heart and spirit are drowned by the clamour of a sort of frenzied restlessness which has become an end in itself, outside the mind's control; its lack of restraint perhaps disguised by a show of callousness or pretended reticence, which is only a sour form of the same sentimentality. Because we no longer value feeling as the God-given language of the spirit, therefore we have become a prey to sentimentality.

If we try to define sentimentality we have to note first that its primary meaning is excessive feeling—feeling given an absolute value—and at the same time feeling in some way contrived and artificial. We expect to find behind an expression of feeling some drama of the soul, but when we look there is only some pitifully limited experience, or even a complete emotional vacuum. The outward forms through which feeling normally finds expression are made use of to arouse an emotional reaction artificially.

A third characteristic of sentimentality is that it lacks humour. The sentimental person is wrapped up in himself;

he wants to gain pleasure from excessive and bogus feeling without paying the price of inward exertion. It is this self-indulgence which makes sentimentality particularly dangerous in the sphere of religion; instead of reverent response to God's grace, there is "pious" feeling; a self-centredness which "already has its reward". Probably in Germany the rise of sentimentality in the eighteenth century is to be connected with Pietism; in England no doubt the contemporary rationalism and horror of "Enthusiasm" made good soil for this and other unfortunate continental influences to breed.

It may be that sentimentality is a more serious danger than kitsch; in our present context, however, what is important is to note that in kitsch sentimentality possesses its most exquisite form of expression; if we are under the influence of sentimentality there is no way of avoiding kitsch.

Tendentiousness and Propaganda in Kitsch

"All art is useless", said Oscar Wilde. If that were so the matter would be quite simple, art ought then to have no ulterior aims. Can it be that this theory gives us another characteristic of kitsch, that it is a concomitant whenever art has an ulterior non-aesthetic purpose? Examples hardly bear this out; the sentimental, pious statue is kitsch without being propaganda, and the works of Dickens and Daumier are art as well as being propaganda.

We have already seen that during the actual process of creation the artist must free himself from all other considerations, that he must concentrate all his powers upon finding the true expression of his inner-image. This does not mean, however, that the artist cannot have a definite aim when he begins, and when he completes his work—so

58

long as this is commensurate with the dignity of the subject in hand, and so long as it does not interfere with the process of artistic creation. That Bach should have wished to provide music to accompany the annunciation of the word of God does not invalidate his work—because the music is equal to the task. But if a man attempts a subject beyond his powers, then his motive—no matter how devout—will ruin his art. Whether the product will then be kitsch is a question which needs further investigation.

Bach's music in self-sufficient, whether or not it is put at the service of worship or evangelization; what about the work of Dickens and Daumier? If we read Jane Austen or look at a Turner painting we are absorbed in the delight of sharing the artist's vision, we forget ourselves altogether as we respond to their art. With artists such as Daumier and Dickens we are also gripped by the power of their art, but for this very reason we are forbidden to lose ourselves here. It is the artistic content itself which calls us out of our aesthetic enjoyment to touch our conscience and demand from us a socially responsible attitude to the world around us. The fact that such work can direct us beyond the sphere of art into practical life does not diminish its artistic worth; indeed this is proved by these particular instances, which still we value as art when the social evils which they denounce are no longer with us. Or to take a modern example, Picasso's *Guernica* is recognized as one of the great works of art of our time, but it is also a passionate protest against inhumanity and tyranny.

If on the other hand a subject is used without respect, if it is made use of without regard for human status, or for aesthetic standards, for some preconceived purpose, then the result may be kitsch. Propaganda films and posters can be kitsch, even when they are not sentimental, if they are spurious; they use art as a means to arouse, through a cheap over-simplification, a particular desired reaction from the public.

We must, moreover, insist that tendentiousness and propaganda within the moral and religious field are already evils in themselves because there is no sphere where short-cuts directed to gaining some particular end are more intrinsically inappropriate. If a priest or teacher, for the sake of making a laudable point, describes a reality without due respect—if for instance he depreciates matrimony in order to extol virginity—or passes over a reality of vital importance, then he is giving way to a dangerous, albeit well-meant tendentiousness. Or again, a parish celebration or school performance may be arranged in which perhaps scenes and personalities from Scripture and Church history are presented, not for their true meaning, or in their historical reality, but as means to some pious end. It may well be that the participants, when they come to reflect afterwards on the presentation and its implications, will feel that they were imposed on, and so become mistrustful of Church practice, even of Christian truth itself. They begin to resent the fact that such one-sided, lazy means were used to promote zeal for the Church.

In all this there may have been no actual kitsch; but the fundamental insincerity and lack of respect for the material used is enough to point the connection. Tendentious propaganda and kitsch invoke one another. From the opposite end we have already seen in Plates 4 and 7 how the technique of propaganda—of "getting at" the beholder —can be used to promote kitsch effects.

Kitsch and Modern Art

Men are apt to consider that kitsch is mainly a woman's world. And of course there is something to be said for this point of view. Emotion plays a greater part in a woman's life, and at a certain depth and inwardness her experience seems to be more vital, personal and beautiful than that of a man, but when her experience remains superficial sense-stimulation is greater, and emotional life slips more easily from one plane to another, the spiritual is apt to be reduced imperceptibly to the sensuous. Thus women often become willing purchasers of religious kitsch in every form.

Because women are by nature more religious (not a weakness but an advantage), they are more active in the religious sphere, and for this very reason pious kitsch is more likely to play a larger part in their lives. But men too buy kitsch pictures and enjoy the dripping sentiment of ultra-pious hymns. Moreover, whereas with women the kitsch which is cherished is almost always straightforward and naïve, with men it is more likely to be calculated, dangerous and vicious in effect.

The form of kitsch which appeals more easily to men has been called "sour". "There are two kinds of kitsch, the sweet and the sour. The sweet you will find in shops selling devotional articles, the sour in art exhibitions."[4] Sour kitsch is distinguished by the form of its presentation, artificial and consciously "contemporary", it favours the abstract, because that "is the way people paint today", and also—though this is not admitted—because it requires less effort. In so far as this is dishonesty in artistic expression it is pure kitsch. This is not in any way to dismiss abstract art as such, but it is no disservice to those who are working seriously to issue a warning against the pseudo-art which attaches itself to this sphere where it is less easily and less quickly seen through.

[4] Paul Fechter in his dictionary of literary terms (*Kleines Wörterbuch für literarische Gespräche*, Gutersloh, 1950), under the heading "Kitsch".

What is Kitsch?

Sour kitsch may, however, derive from a whole attitude to life, as well as from current art-forms. Hans Egon Holthusen has pointed out that today alongside the kitsch tendency to sugarcoat the world, there is also a sentimental bent towards darkening reality, reducing it to crude realism, a nihilism which is destructive of all affirmative values in such work. The producer of sour kitsch, says Holthusen, works on the principle "Praised be that which causes pain".[5] The element of kitsch lies in the fact that the artist's subject is not seen as an authentic inner-image, but is obscured by negative wishful thinking, and the form given to it is painted far too easily in the blackest, crudest colours, with an almost gleeful cruelty towards himself and his contemporaries. Holthusen rightly sees a reason for this in the fact that young artists particularly choose as the subject of their work the terrifying problems of the war-time, and post-war world, and the menace of the atom bomb, when humanly and artistically they have not the stature or maturity to meet their theme. So the works they produce are inadequate and they themselves, having once set foot upon the slippery slope of bogus and inadequate artistic expression, easily debase their genuine talent.

In our own experience this sort of kitsch has not yet perhaps appeared in religious art except maybe in the bitter paintings of the Indian de Souza, but it is easily recognizable in other fields and is certainly a very present danger. The cheaper sort of vaguely abstract, by-way-of being modern art is illustrated in Plate 17.

Kitsch and the Man in the Street

Is the intellectual or the owner of a Jaguar better pro-

[5] H. E. Holthusen, *Ja und Nein. Neue kritische Versuche* (Munich, 1954), pp. 242 ff.

ected against kitsch than the farm labourer or the manual worker? We know from experience that the answer to his question is not an unreserved "yes". It is, however, a act that individual members of a nation share, to varying legrees and in different ways, in a common cultural eritage. Some are aware, some give it very little thought, nd some share only in the utilitarian content of the common life or are content with the remains of a cultural ontent abandoned by the intellectual leaders, who are lready interested in new experience and new forms of xpression.

When we speak of "the man in the street" or "the eople", we mean those who from the scientific and artstic points of view receive, and use, in distinction from hose in a community who intellectually select, or create. he expression naturally covers a great range of individuals, and the farm or manual worker may live more fully n a worthy tradition, and be more at home in his cultural nvironment than the half-educated graduate whose interests have hardly gone beyond the problem of earning living and what he can comfortably assimilate from the ewspaper, the radio, or public house talk. The order of lescent is not "educated, half-educated, ordinary people", ut "educated, half-educated, mentally stagnant" on down o mentally defective. The "people", in the sense in which he term is used here, means those who are not yet fully ducated, not yet masters of their own cultural heritage, it neans the masses; but it must always be remembered that he health and the cultural force of nations is rooted in the nasses, it is from them that again and again the creative ersonalities emerge. Certainly the poor in spirit, the intellectually unpretentious, those whom our Lord especially oved and declared holy in the Sermon on the Mount, were f "the people". And as human beings these rank above

the pretentious half-educated; this distinction is essentia
in the discussion of kitsch.

Kitsch and the man in the street: we must not expec
too much. Most people, from the simplest well up into
academic circles, love kitsch, especially naïve straight
forward kitsch. Why? One reason lies in the attraction of
the subject, of that which is represented, in the kitsch
work. A person's artistic perception is not something isola
ted; he is also curious, interested in facts, emotionally at
tached to people, involved in things and memories, subject
to impulses and anticipations in imagination; faced with a
work of art his reaction may be to consider its utility and
the practical value, etc.; in a word it may affect him from
all sorts of points of view. The simpler the person is, the
less differentiated in his mental life, the more likely he
is to think solely about the subject of a picture or poem
He will hardly notice the form through which he is made
aware of this content, and because of this overriding in
terest in content he will prefer the form of expression
which speaks loudest, and which requires least attention
and trouble on his part. Insofar as the viewer or listener is
directly gripped by the subject of a piece of kitsch, his
reaction will be strong and enjoyable, despite the bogus
form. In course of time, this poison in the form will
gnaw away at his character; but that is another question
to be considered later.

A second explanation of the popularity of kitsch is that
the ordinary man likes the compelling language of the
senses, flat bright colours, and strong tunes, and to a large
extent he is right. When life is dull and monotonous men
need a strong stimulant.

We are introduced here to the element of relativity in
kitsch and the experience of kitsch; it is bound to vary in
quality and degree according to the experience and the

environment of each individual. Brilliant colours in clothes may look beautiful among fields of corn in the summer sunshine, and garish in the city office. The factory worker may also like gaudy colours, not because they go with his environment, but as an instinctive protest against drabness and inhumanity. The naïve simplicity which is adapted to one kind of life, and seems beautiful there, may give the impression of mere clumsiness elsewhere. A Tyrolean Christmas yodelling hymn is an authentic and beautiful expression of peasant devotion; but if it is sung at a parochial concert or even at a city Midnight Mass, it gives an effect of artificiality, not of art. Those who sing it have to adapt themselves to forms of expression belonging to a quite different way of life; it is not for them the spontaneous and natural expression of their own piety, and so something bogus easily slips in and they begin to feel at home and enjoy themselves in this alien costume. Or, to take an opposite case, an ill-trained amateur orchestra may try to play a movement from a symphony by Mozart or Beethoven; the result is bound to be not only barbarous but kitsch because when both musical experience and technical ability are lacking there can be no spontaneity in music-making. The players are not in fact wanting to make music so much as to see themselves in the role of this or that philharmonic orchestra.

Kitsch may be relative, its enjoyment by simple people may be easy to explain, but this still does not mean that the cheap and dubious element in it is not there, or that it is not still dangerous.

Is there no alternative? Is it not possible for the man in the street to appreciate spiritual values through genuine contemporary art-forms? Here appears a third reason for the popularity of kitsch. When the manual crafts were largely displaced by machine-production in the industrial

revolution, educated people, those who ought to have
heard the call of their time, neglected to make use of the
new techniques to create, or help the people create for
themselves, new popular arts to replace the old traditions.[6]
The fabricators of kitsch were able to step into the breach
and set up in business.

Devastated land has to be reclaimed and brought back
into cultivation. Making the art of the past available
through reproduction by mechanical processes is like put-
ting vases of cut flowers on a barren field. As long as there
is no other way this must be done, and it is the experience
of publishers and others that by this means it is possible
to shut out much which is inferior, and to create a true
appreciation of art; but this will not lead people back into
their lost paradise. Only a vital, contemporary art can do
that. And the need is well-known, at least to many artists;
I am not thinking of the beatnik scribblers and pop-artists,
but of those who are really distressed at being estranged
from the people. Such artists are painfully aware of the
gulf created by different ways of thought, and by the unfortunate receptiveness to kitsch of the aesthetically naïve
masses. They long to speak in a language intelligible to all,
and at the same time they know that they must also be
true to their own inspiration, that any solution which involves a betrayal of their art can only be a blind alley.
They need to go on trying, searching for means to understand and to meet the rightful needs of the people.
Perhaps great artists will come, who can invent a new
language, both intelligible and artistically true. Perhaps

[6] This accusation cannot justifiably be made of Britain. The pro-
moters of the Great Exhibition of 1851, and the founders of the
Victoria and Albert Museum, men like the Prince Consort, Sir Henry
Cole, Owen Jones, were very much aware of this problem and made
great efforts to find solutions. Perhaps this is why kitsch has on the
whole been much less widespread in England than in Germany.

in Rouault, Epstein and Graham Sutherland we already
have such artists at work; certainly the growing popularity of modern art exhibitions, the unprecedented attraction of Coventry Cathedral with its works of modern
religious art, are a hopeful sign.

We must not, however, allow ourselves to form a sentimental idea of the good "ordinary people". It is realistic
to talk of the "masses"; there is no question today of the
native sensitivity of a primitive people. We have instead a
brash pseudo-culture particularly favourable to evil kitsch.
Great effort on both sides will be needed if we are to
achieve a new art of the people.

Children and Kitsch

We have to begin at the beginning. The child is drawn
to colour, noise, movement, sensation, simplification, even
more powerfully than the man in the street; and unfortunately he finds these in kitsch. For just as he does not
distinguish between fantasy and reality, but uses simplify-
ing fairy tales and magnifying imaginative fabrications in
order gradually to come to a grasp of reality, in the same
way he seizes on the strong colours and simplified forms
of kitsch and does not recognize that they are bogus and
cheap because his normal experience is pre-artistic. It is
only gradually, as he grows and learns, that he begins to
acquire the faculty to distinguish the true and the genuine
in art. In a weakened and somewhat altered form this process can still be observed in the young adolescent.

We can and should find and offer to children toys,
books, forms of expression, which give them what they
need, without being kitsch. But it is unwise to make fun
of their taste, this may indeed have the opposite effect
and confirm their worst traits. This is something which has

always to be kept in mind by those who want to free people from kitsch. In particular it would be criminal to rob a simple person of valuable spiritual experience and understanding, because at the moment his only access to these is through deplorable forms. This is particularly important in pastoral work; better a genuine devotion to our Lady through a hymn or picture which is kitsch than no devotion at all. But this does not mean that we are justified in allowing things to go on as they are; there is a serious danger both to those who (still) possess the Marian experience, and to those who do not (yet) possess it, specifically because of the repulsive forms of kitsch in which so often it is presented to us. It is a dilemma : what matters with the Church is religious content; she has to find forms of expression for this suited to the capacity of her members; yet it may be that artistic means are not at her disposal. The Church has at various times, in particular countries, been almost compelled to make use of kitsch. There have, on the other hand, been pastors of souls who have had the choice between kitsch and art, and who have chosen kitsch. Wherever either of these things happens it indicates some neglect in the education of both priest and people. It is not by accident that genuine art-forms are lacking for pastoral work; nor is it accidental that many pastors refuse to admit the difference between the kitsch and the genuine; both are symptoms of a deeper crisis, to which we shall return.

The Art-Historical Background

Catholic art in Protestant countries has been largely an importation from those countries which remained Catholic after the Reformation; certainly most of the kitsch pictures and statues sold in Britain are imported. The historical process by which the art of these countries deteriorated into kitsch is therefore relevant to our understanding of the stuff which has appealed so disastrously to Catholic taste or sentiment everywhere, even though it is not relevant to the history of our own art.

Historically, the roots of modern kitsch are in the Baroque and Rococo styles of the seventeenth and eighteenth centuries. The motive force of this style is the idea that "through sensuous suggestion, at supreme levels we can attain immediate perception of the supra-sensible; and conversely that it is only in the purest and most extreme of sensuous terms that the likeness and form of the supra-sensible is conveyed—this may be a paradox; but it is the tension involved in this idea which is the principle of a style which is exuberantly rich and was immensely fruitful."[7] If we apply the theological principle that grace presupposes nature, then a paradox of this kind is not only possible but necessary. It has been said that it is precisely at the moments of most intense physical experience, in erotic ecstasy and in death, that man becomes directly certain of the existence of God. This is true even if few men rise to such heights of experience; and it is this experience which Bernini, perhaps the greatest of Baroque religious artists, has evoked in his *St Teresa in Ecstasy*. Here the supernatural is expressed in a blazingly sensuous erotic symbol, analogous to the erotic language used by mystics of all ages. There is no kitsch in Bernini, but the language which he uses derives from the dynamism, the universality, and lack of inhibition, of the piety of Baroque Rome. We live in a very different world today. Nor is Bernini the only Baroque artist. In others, the tension is not so high; or it may be that the treatment is on an altogether different plane, as in Plate 13, or maybe

[7] Wilhelm Hausenstein, *Essay über den Kitsch* (Anm. 1).

the change in atmosphere from our own is too great and
the fault can be in our response, which is certainly affected
by the artistic productions of the intervening periods.

On the Continent Baroque was followed by Rococo, the
last truly great art-epoch of the German-speaking
countries. Again, it would be absurd to think of kitsch in
connection with Mozart, the brothers Zimmerman, Bal-
thasar Neuman, or Ignaz Günther. Nevertheless, it is
relevant to ask whether there is not something in the
special character of this period, its means of expression,
and perhaps also its form of experience, which did not
render it liable to slide into kitsch; or at least make it
unable to stem or divert the process which finally led to
artistic infertility and kitsch.

For the rococo artist illusionism was itself a style-
medium. This has nothing to do with kitsch or spuriousness. The dynamism of the drive towards formal expression was so great that normal means of expression were no
longer apt. The heaven storming jubilation could not be
translated into mere stone; it needed also the theatrical
devices, used for instance in the Wieskirche; or imitations
of marble (if real were not available) might be used to
create atmosphere and effect through colour and colour
interplay. As long as this was the expression of compelling
inward dynamism it was true to itself, but in the hands of
those lacking real artistic inspiration the temptation to
flirt with these infinitely adaptable forms and devices is
irresistible. When the true artist let himself go, or when
the charlatan or bungler was at work rococo, forms easily
cease to correspond to any values, become merely pleasurable playthings—and so very near to kitsch.

With illusionism is also connected the almost intoxi-
cated character of the rococo style. If we think of the
architectonic configuration of a rococo altar, what glow-

ing fantasy, what exuberance of feeling do we not find; we are caught up into the heavenward surge and ecstatic bliss of these enraptured saints, eddying clouds and dancing drapery. Obviously, it is very easy in this situation to fall into personal illusions, to slide from one plane of values into another, even in the last resort to confuse heavenly and sensuous bliss.

The rococo was also the age of pastoral romance, of sentimental hermitages, and coquettish saints. Feuchtmayr's statue of the Madonna (Plate 18) has been called blasphemous for its pose, the revealing lines of the dress, and realistic treatment of the face. This is unjust, a rococo figure cannot be treated apart from its setting, but still there is here a definite secularization of a religious subject; and so we meet another dangerous element in rococo. "Heaven and earth are seen as one, religious feeling takes on the forms of feelings of earthly love."[8] We have here an ambivalence which in any case is a danger; it is obviously easy in this way to experience as kitsch what is genuine art. Müller-Erb has suggested kitsch is normally found as a transitional phenomenon at the beginning and end of every stylistic epoch. His thesis is that at a time when there are new impulses, which like new wine do not fit into the old flasks of earlier styles, then we are likely to get art forms which are unbalanced, emotionally charged, bizarre. He instances Carolingian art which seems almost to burst the inherited forms of late antique art in its energy and excitement. In this case the new impulse was accepted and the old forms transformed, but it may be that instead of acceptance the impulse arouses fear, so that people cling to an out-dated form and thus slip into infantile decadence; what happens is known to depth-psychology as

---

[8] Heinrich Lützeler, *Die christliche Kunst des Abendlandes*, Bonn, 1932, pp. 194f.

regression, which being an unnatural, defective approach easily leads to kitsch. An English example would be the academic art of this century. A great deal of kitsch, though not mostly religious, has been exhibited at the Royal Academy from *Alma-Tadema* onwards. The rococo marks the end of the magnificent art-epoch which began with the Renaissance; an art epoch when, more prominently than ever before, the secular appears alongside the sacred, sometimes indeed penetrating it so that only the façade of religious art is left. So we arrive at the courtly decadence of some rococo madonnas, and thence at a religious art which as it comes towards its final period, while not yet kitsch, is also not quite genuine.

We must also keep in mind the sociological background. The French Revolution was already imminent; the ruling classes tended to take refuge from the crisis which they could not ignore, in the forced naivety of pastoral poetry. A generation too weak to abandon an outworn way of life was equally unable to renew the vitality of Baroque and Rococo inspired as these had been by the now waning religious force of the Counter-Reformation. Its life remained on the surface, clinging to the charm of outward forms of artistic expression.

Meanwhile, the Age of Enlightenment had arrived; the most influential minds in Europe were inspired by rationalism and advocated a rationalist and utilitarian morality. The last great rococo artists had sufficient vitality to adapt themselves to the new mood and the transition to the classical style is therefore gradual; but the repudiation of the emotional side of human nature in the rationalist philosophy resulted also in another form of artistic expression —the reaction of the Romantic movement. Romanticism, which is the most dangerous of all the diseases liable to threaten the German people, is always to some extent a departure, if not a flight from reality. In this case where it sprang from the depths of the subconscious it took dangerously distorted forms, and finally gained a no less dangerous recognition.

Nineteenth-century kitsch does not derive directly from rococo, but from the final stages of this double-faced romantic-classical movement which succeeded it. In the second half of the century the bourgeosie were sheltering themselves from the claims of the working classes in a cheap paradise. The conditions of the time almost cried out for kitsch, and so it gained a total dominion which has no historical parallel.

This German background, which corresponds neither politically nor artistically to contemporary development in England, made the importation of German religious art particularly disastrous. England had no native Baroque or Rococo as a basis or inspiration; the eighteenth century had indeed been almost completely barren in religious art. Moreover, the expanding Catholic Church of the nineteenth century, looking for visual means of teaching and inculcating piety, turned also to another, equally decadent source, from France.[9]

[9] The history of religious art in England and its link-up with the Continent is outlined on p. 150. *The Old Testament in Art* and *The Gospels in Art*, edited by W. Shaw Sparrow, will provide the interested reader with illustrations of late nineteenth-century Continental religious painting, its English counterpart and its Raphaelesque prototypes.

V

The Breeding Ground of Kitsch and its Moral Effects

WE have seen where kitsch is liable to find its way into the process of artistic creation and enjoyment. Let us now consider it from the other end, from the point of view of the man, and his moral and spiritual life.

Original Sin

None of us is magically protected from kitsch. Not only may we fall foul in matters of art, but we are also liable to do the same thing spiritually, and take refuge in similar types of experience. The theologian sees the roots of this in original sin.

Even the redeemed feel the effects of original sin. Harmony between different levels of life and instinct, established by grace, are liable to be destroyed in us by original sin; concupiscence or inordinate desire becomes particularly and painfully obvious in the conflict between spirit and flesh. (For a proper appreciation of art it is important to realize that the biblical expressions "flesh" and "spirit" are not to be identified with our modern concepts of body and soul-spirit; in the New Testament both words specifically describe the whole man, the one in the order of damnation, the other in that of salvation.)

Art of its very nature demands that there should be harmony between spiritual values and the experience of their sensible expression; for this reason, the disorder caused by original sin is liable particularly to offset it. All art is of the senses; and generally also sensually enjoyable. The disorder of original sin is likely, therefore, to introduce an unbalanced emphasis on the sensible and its promise of pleasure. Dishonesty is very liable to creep in where someone's personal response to the spiritual values of the artist's inspiration are distorted.

The passive receptive element in aesthetic experience provides another danger for both the creator and the beholder or listener. For the latter there is an opening for sloth and mere pleasure seeking, which becomes dishonest when the pretext of an aesthetic response is maintained. For the artist, the fact that the creative process involves an element of fantasy, even of intoxication, before the starting-point of his inspiration is transformed, its inner value captured, means that, as a result of original sin, the artist can easily lapse into a dream world. For from both artist and beholder, art, as we have seen, demands effort and seriousness; when this is not made, artistic activity becomes a flight from reality. It can become not only a bogus reflection of reality but an opening for the devil. Satan can present himself as an angel of light more strikingly, and much more easily, in an artistic symbol than in a scientific concept.

Timidity and Emotional Immaturity

In our present world artistic experience is always in danger of misleading us and of falsifying reality. Even one who lives in the mind and truth of Christ, even he "who thinks he stands firmly should beware of a fall" (1 Cor. 10.12). Pious timidity or lack of flexibility may try to avoid the difficulties by taking short-cuts. To do this is to abandon God's gift of art in pusillanimous fear; it is falling into the error of Tertullian when he says, "Where virtue rules, beauty is of no account; for beauty properly speaking serves only to rouse sensual pleasure."

We are all subject to the effects of original sin, but in practice some temperaments are more open to the particular dangers of kitsch than others. To begin with, true appreciation of art demands a "big and simple heart", it demands a capacity for profound experience, a certain degree of emotional depth and maturity, the power to feel the great as great, the pure as pure, the profound as profound. Some people lack such a capacity; the mental defective, the psychopath with a feeble emotional response, people who are inadequately gifted in this field, these are liable to have no idea of the nature of a real response to art, and are therefore more or less without the power to resist kitsch.

It may be, however, that a disposition to kitsch is accounted for not so much by lack of capacity to respond to art as by arrested development, inadequate education, or by the weariness of the absorbing struggle to gain a bare livelihood. Modern depth-psychology has shown the disastrous effect of such conditions. For us it is relevant that an undeveloped or repressed emotional life presents an ideal breeding ground for kitsch. We have already touched on this problem in relation to sentimentality and noted the modern atrophy of feeling, which is particularly liable to affect religious life by exposing it frequently to kitsch. It is sad to see this ascendancy of sentimentality as it grows in the life of the individual. Religious life becomes poverty-stricken and egocentric, and we tend to belittle the importance of truth in our faith and to lose the idea of piety as a direct face-to-face encounter with God. As these attitudes gain ascendancy in our minds, so we come more and more to misplace the focal point of religion in relation to our emotional lives. People who are cool and calculating in practical life, who pursue their political and economic aims with ruthless logic, think that their religious lives should be governed by feeling only. The result of these demands on their already stunted emotional resources is sentimentality, and this seizes upon every form of kitsch which it encounters.

The same emotional weakening of religious life may be found among simple devout people for whom piety may virtually take over the whole of their active life, so that other interests are undeveloped or atrophied through neglect. They naturally expect some return from this piety; what more natural than that they should give way to kitsch which offers so many opportunities of sentimental satisfaction to those who expect little of life?

Repressed Sex

Religious kitsch proliferates especially when the world of sexual love is not known, accepted, and built into our personal life in its God-willed bodiliness, and this is so even when it is precisely for religion's sake that sex has been repressed—instead of having been sacrificed with open eyes. Bert Herzog, who deserves credit for having demonstrated the subconscious influences in the origin of kitsch, has expressed himself forcefully on this point: "I may be allowed to point to one piece of kitsch which even today infects ninety out of a hundred churches; that horror, painted, carved, or made of plaster, which is called 'the Virgin Mary', 'the Immaculate Conception', 'Our Lady of Lourdes', and so on. It is in fact not accidental that Mary here almost always appears as a sweet girl, more precisely as a curious combination of courtesan and goddess, for these images make manifest nothing of Mary the Mother of God, but rather (although this is naturally not admitted and is often also unconscious) the feminine part of man's soul—still in a primitive state—his undifferentiated anima. If we consider coolly these dolls made of marzipan and cosmetics looking upward with cowlike glances supposed to be 'soulful', this artificial set-up, this excessive affectation, behind which a lascivious element often lurks, then we can perceive more or less exactly the secret idea which many men have of the feminine nature. And indeed, those who produce and buy this kitsch are for the most part men, parish priests and church leaders—in this respect it is significant that modern Marian kitsch often resembles to a hair's breadth certain film stars, even to the rosy painted kissable lips. Amazingly little survives here of theology and of the fine distinctions of nearly two thousand years of Mariology; I have always been surprised that priests who have been trained in theology, not only themselves enjoy such products of a corrupt and perverted religious outlook, but also commend them to the devotion of the faithful. We must ask ourselves: What will these souls look like after they have been devastated by such pictures of the Mother of God? and what does the charge 'care of souls' mean in this respect . . . ?"[1] These are very strong words, but are we sure that we can maintain that the author is wholly wrong?

We cannot fail to recognize the importance of such (depth) psychological reflections. We might naturally point also to the often repressed *animus* function in woman, which leads her also, in the religious sphere, to the choice of a picture of Christ which is kitsch.

Religious Decadence

It is not only an unbalanced emotional life which opens

[1] "Religiöser Kitsch", *Orientierung*, 1950, 11, pp. 228f.

the door to kitsch in religion, but also neglect of religious life itself. A person who has never in his own soul confronted the Godhead, who has not, in more precise terms, encountered the (triune) personality of God in a direct (I-Thou) relationship, cannot grasp the depths of reality. One who does not fully comprehend the indispensability of moral norms will be defenceless against the falsifying of artistic experience through kitsch—particularly where it purports to be religious art. Not that this is necessarily the fault of the individual; the religion of a whole age can be metaphysically shallow.

In fact, since the Middle Ages, as a result of increasing individualism, religious experience has become more and more superficial. Its focal point has moved away from the profound centre of the sacred mysteries into peripheral areas of subjective feelings and beyond that to sentimental devotions. As people lost their understanding of the depth of the liturgical mysteries, they lost also their power to use the language of sacred symbols. Religious art lost its symbolic character. If we consider the transition from the majesty of the Romanesque church, planned for communal worship, through the religious individualism reflected in the crown of ambulatory chapels so typical of the Gothic cathedral, to the rococo hermitage and the Lourdes grotto of the nineteenth century, we realize the long distance that we have travelled. When religion itself is no longer capable of making people aware of the immensity of its measure, they are almost bound to be taken in by kitsch.

Collectivization

Today this danger is overshadowed by an even greater; the metaphysical shallowness induced by the collectiviza-

What is Kitsch?

tion of all our activities. All standardization, particularly when it is a levelling down, is at the expense of the individual personality, and means that life grows shallower more impoverished. Collective man is concerned with the utilitarian and the pleasurable, not with the life of the spirit. The danger of kitsch is overshadowed by the sinister danger of a blindness to all those values which make life worth living, a blindness which may become complete Naturally a life so superficial, so adapted to utility and pleasure will be wide open to all forms of kitsch; but, compared with the truly diabolical despoiling of humanity in collectivization this is a slight evil. Were this process successful, there would no longer be any point in fighting against kitsch; but so long as it is in the balance the fight is worth while, because it constantly brings up and proclaims true, the metaphysical depths of human existence The fight against kitsch helps to prevent life becoming depersonalized and entirely superficial; it is therefore also part of the fight to save our lives from the threat of collectivization and its attendant stagnation.

Unbalanced Extremes in the Understanding of Art

We have already referred to those who seem to lack any gift for the understanding of art, and we shall return to this, but let us first consider at the other end of the scale those who idolize beauty. "Beauty is everywhere around us . . . it is a strange flower and blooms in the most unlikely places, but whatever the soil, once it burgeons it can hardly be destroyed. Remove it from one spot and it will blossom in another, and often in the least considered place. It is proper to mankind alone and it magnifies the man who kneels before it, pouring into his trembling and ecstatic heart all the things that make the life of man worth while." With these words, Adalbert Stifter, in his *Brigitta*, makes clear that we have in beauty a mysterious, primitive datum which pervades all human fields of value, which cannot be fully grasped by means of logical thought or conceptual analysis, or reduced to values of another order—moral values, for instance. And here we have two dangers. The first we have already mentioned; idolization of the beautiful. Delight in beauty can be so intoxicating that we go no further, we allow it to prevent and waylay us in our search for God, instead of leading us to him, its source. As St Augustine wrote, "The eyes love fair and varied forms, bright and soft colours. Let not these occupy my soul; let God rather occupy it who made these things, very good indeed, yet he is my good, not they." We have noted the error of the doctrine of art for art's sake. Morally the danger of allowing aesthetic values to absorb those of holiness and morality is obvious. In relation to kitsch the greatest danger is social. People, particularly teachers, who transmit the intoxication of their own experience to others who are less gifted, and incapable of the same response, expose the latter to the lure of kitsch.

Today our mood is perhaps too disillusioned for this to be a great temptation, we may associate it more with the aestheticism of the nineties. But an obvious contemporary example is to be found in the aesthetic approach to the liturgy, with its tendency to regard the beauty of ritual and music as something complete in itself—an approach which is perhaps more common outside than inside the Church. Outside the Church, among those at sea in a world of shifting values, where nothing is secure or true, art is often felt to be the one valid experience, since its validity is self-subsistent and independent of all outside considerations. As a beginning, this is the recognition of art as a saving God-given gift to man in periods of doubt and fear, a personal contact with the true and the real. But the sophisticated "pop-art" of today, in its deliberate frivolity, is surely an example of a refusal to go beyond art, a turning back of art upon itself, denying its spiritual mission; and therefore kitsch.

The second danger for the gifted is with those who may be highly educated and intelligent, but who have no understanding of the language of beauty. Lack of balance between the superior level of the rest of their lives and their complete lack in this respect predestines them to kitsch. They often mistake the purpose of art, considering it as meant merely to provide pleasure and relaxation, as in fact an extra, fundamentally unnecessary. Beauty takes its revenge on these masters of sober thought and upright will (one cannot help thinking of senior British civil servants), and entices them to a plane that lies far below the art to which they give only lip service, namely to the plane of kitsch. Such people will look at a work of art very probably seeing only its subject and passing from this, not to the inner image of the artist, but to their own related interests and associations—possibly even trying to find in it ethical, religious or political ideas, regardless of the intention of the artist. Judgment may be given, not on artistic content, but on skill and technique, whether the grapes are so real that a bird might peck them, or on failure to reach such a standard of realism, when it may not have been in any way what the artist wanted to do. To take an extreme example, suppose someone lacking in all aesthetic appreciation were to stand before Michelangelo's *Creation of Adam* in the Sistine Chapel; he would be blind to the beauty of the fresco, and therefore fail to be touched inwardly by the unique evocation of man's creatureliness; to him it would be just a representation of a naked body, in the same class as an anatomical drawing or a photograph from the life; instead of responding to the wonderful relationship between this living form and its Creator, he might have to cope with erotic-sexual suggestions.

In this extreme example we can perhaps see just what is really involved. The man who lacks aesthetic sensibility will be in danger because he will see only what is on the surface, only the representational aspect of a work of art and its associations. He may find a superficial charm in these and so enjoy a trashy experience and become involved in kitsch.

The causes of these types of aesthetic failure would seem to be four. It may lie in a person's psycho-physical make-up; he may be tone-deaf, or colour blind, or blind to the beauty of form, in varying degrees. Or it may be in lack of imagination, or lack of imaginative experience, through lack of opportunity. Here clearly those who are gifted and fortunate can help those who need to be shown the way, to be fired by others, before they can begin to see the deeper meaning and beauty embodied in the sensible forms of art. Thirdly, the capacity may be there, but retarded in its development by false ideas, perhaps owing to a very active way of life in scientific, technical or educational work, and sometimes a wrong approach to asceticism. We have to be humble and accept the importance, the necessity of leisure, and the duty to respond to the infinite riches of God and his creation. Work directed to good and useful ends is still inferior and incomplete without the creative work which God also has required and empowered men to do. Finally, there may be real value-blindness to art, and then there is nothing for it but honest humble resignation. Such people may be called to sublime learning, to activity of social importance, to holiness, but they must be silent in the face of beauty which they cannot understand, and not allow an intellectual acquaintance with art to delude them (or others) into thinking that they have had an experience which is in fact denied to them. When they are in charge of cultural affairs their most seemly attitude is to refrain from interfering, and generously to leave the task to those with the vocation.

Self-indulgence

Beyond the lack of capacity for true artistic experience —for whatever cause—there lies the case of the person who has lost his capacity through self-indulgence. Someone who has never learnt to accept life as it is, who will not face up to the fact that it is only by self-mastery that we enter into the order of reality, someone who has never learned a self-forgetting approach to another person, but who instead relates everything to himself, making it serve his own interests; such a man will treat beauty in the same way, and will be particularly open to kitsch. "There are people who are pleased with the trivial, sentimental, sweetly tasteless, cheaply effective, sensational, and who look for these qualities in art. The noble and profound quality of true art, which avoids all cheap effects, does not appeal to them and is not able to arouse their enthusiasm . . . it is not merely that they look for something in art which does not belong to art but to another sphere of life, but that they look for qualities which are negative and perverted also in life" (Dietrich von Hildebrand).

The only hope in such a case is complete change of heart.

VI

Moral Ineptitude as the Heart of Kitsch

WE must take up a question which has constantly recurred in our analysis. It seems that it is more exact to describe kitsch as morally valueless than as lacking beauty. Because kitsch always claims to appear in the guise of the beautiful, it has been thought of as something which belongs in the aesthetic sphere, which can therefore be just set aside, with indignation perhaps, possibly just with a rueful or contemptuous smile. Too little notice has been taken of the way in which it can contribute to moral breakdown. And in this respect straightforward kitsch is particularly dubious because it may not be realized as such; and so its work of moral attrition goes on unnoticed. The reason for this under-estimation of the power of kitsch is often due to a blindness to the value of beauty and its importance for the morally good and devout life. Those who fail to appreciate beauty will fail also to see the full significance of its corruption.

Untruthfulness, Irreverence, Shamelessness

As soon as we look at kitsch from the ethical point of view its deceitfulness becomes obvious. A kitsch product presents itself as the artistic rendering of something real. In the same way a kitsch experience is one which assumes that the true value-content of a work of art has been grasped. Whereas in neither case has there been any personal achievement of this kind, but something inferior; the claim is bogus.

We normally apply the words "bogus" and "spurious" in the first instance to things. Do they also necessarily have a moral implication? In characteristic kitsch—such as the plaster statues of our Lady of Lourdes—we have work which deliberately represents something different from the supposed subject. (We have Bernadette's testimony that they are historically untrue: "My lady was much more natural and not a bit tired-looking; she wasn't praying all the time.") In these images someone has aimed at producing an attractive female form under the pretext of religion, whether from frivolous irresponsibility or in calculating a more favourable market. The dishonesty may not be conscious; in straightforward kitsch the devout artist may be unaware of the bogus quality of his work because its roots are in his whole attitude to life. The typical "Immaculate Virgin" does not represent any religious reality; the holiness or virginity, suggested by a lily perhaps or some other outward sign, is not present in any spiritual sense in the artist's conception. Here is a spuriousness which is based on a more or less conscious untruthfulness. What the artist conceals from himself, or from others, what he seeks to promote deliberately or otherwise, behind the bogus façade, is very often sensual pleasure.

If a work of art is used not for beauty, its specific quality, but for some other lower purpose, then there is irreverence, even if the other purpose is by way of being in the service of morality and religion. All kitsch is irreverent, no matter how pious it claims to be, because it abuses or parodies the proper values of art.

Everything has its own value; if this is ignored, or if

man uses it as a means to some other end, then he is irreverent. With lesser values this may be excused on grounds of inattentiveness; it is easy to overlook a daisy. But with the higher value of beauty, this irreverence is patently an offence against God, the Creator and primal essence of the beautiful. It is the first step to the sin of pride, to the self-glorification and self-sufficiency of the creature. When a man no longer looks around him to notice the wonder of created things, or does not trouble to respond to them; when he ignores real values in order to devote himself to his own interests and desires, he is already on the point of revolting against God. Such irreverence is particularly liable to occur in the field of art, and it is not only the pleasure seeker who is at risk, but paradoxically also his opposite, the moral zealot. The puritan, who is so strict in maintaining moral standards, is apt to be proportionately lax in his attention to the divine message which art transmits. By the irony of divine wisdom, his punishment for not wishing to accept the validity of a language which makes use of the senses, is that he will probably have a special weakness for kitsch, and so unconsciously abandon himself to sensuous pleasure.

In the enjoyment of kitsch there is concealed yet another form of poison which touches on the very nerve of human dignity, namely, its lack of shame. Whenever anything intimate takes place, not only in matters of sex, whether it concerns the body or the soul, the question of modesty or shame arises. When we realize the all-penetrating function of shame in human life, the shamelessness of kitsch becomes apparent. It is most evident when we let ourselves go and give ourselves away in our reaction to a kitsch hymn or representation. Someone who sings a hymn in a sentimental way is not ashamed of showing how much he enjoys the pleasure of cheap raptures and "tender" melancholy. It is disgraceful to abandon oneself to such enjoyment, and shaming to do it in public.

This becomes even more serious when something of high intrinsic value is misused; when, for instance, what should be a hymn of homage to God is used as a pretext for pleasure or quick educational results—when a priest says, "I do not care whether the hymn is good art or worthless, so long as it stirs people in the way I want." In such a case philistine obtuseness sacrifices true religious experience by seeking a utilitarian short-cut; the intimate personal relationship between God and the soul (which belongs to God alone) should only be realized in the presence of others in the reverence and seriousness of liturgical action : instead it is paraded in public. Humanly speaking, we ought to be ashamed not only before God, but for God, if for the sake of pleasure or of a quick pastoral success we use kitsch to express or exploit a religious experience. Is God in this way to be stripped of his majesty before man ? Can we speak of the fear of God or of the love of God when all that we mean is pleasure or success ? A person who sacrifices God's majesty in religious kitsch does so hypocritically, in the name of reverence and charity; he is more shameless than the executioners on Calvary, for when they tore our Lord's clothes from his body, they did so at least in the name of retributive justice. In this, as in other ways, it is also easy to fall into kitsch without being consciously aware of the lack of modesty involved.

Duplicity is perhaps the most striking of the ethical characteristics of kitsch, and lack of self-respect its most repulsive. But the most dangerous and the most deep rooted derives from sloth. Kitsch acts like an anaesthetic and is sought after for that reason; one can sink into cosy enjoyment reassured by the cliché, while capacity for personal life at a deeper level atrophies. Real appreciation of art is far removed from this lazy passivity; it demands a response from the whole personality, an affirmation from the heart.

Thus, in the experience of kitsch is concealed the capital sin of *acedia*, sloth, which makes us fretfully turn away from what leads to God, from the world of spiritual things, from the truly beautiful, good and holy, and in the last resort from supernatural grace, because all these things cost effort. They demand an impetus of the will, and a selfless opening of the mind to the real and the true. This refusal involves a stubborn resistance, if not an actual opposition, to the will of God, for a person who abandons himself to kitsch cannot respond with his whole heart to God's love. He is rejecting the gracious but demanding claim made upon him through the beautiful, by that love. From the ethical standpoint, the most devastating thing that can be said of kitsch is that, at bottom, it is a rejection of God.

"Surely kitsch is not as bad as this?" Such might well be the first comment on these reflections. And it is true that in ordinary kitsch there is no actual or complete turning away from God, no mortal sin. Nevertheless, the fact that many devout Christians and some otherwise zealous clergy thoughtlessly treat it as a matter of indifference is disturbing. For it is precisely through small doses of poison that sloth works in the long run, breaking down moral resistance or at least the courage to build up a morally and religiously integrated personality. What has happened to the sluggish soul only becomes apparent when a serious moral crisis arises. Then the consequences of a diet of kitsch become apparent; they deserve a section to themselves.

What is Kitsch?

The Devastating Effects of Kitsch

For most people the realm of art lies on the periphery of their existence and interest. Should their approach to art be mistaken, it still does not seem important to their life as a whole. A capable and devout housewife who busies herself day in day out with her family can surely be forgiven if in one of her rare moments of leisure she reads a kitsch edifying book, or if she keeps holy pictures in her prayer book—which remind her perhaps of the dead, or of the first communion of one of her children. Is an office or manual worker who puts his whole heart into his work, not entitled at the end of the day to enjoy a sentimental film? Even if it is trash, surely, since it is not connected with his "real" life, there is no need to protest. Certainly we must respect the freedom of our fellow-men with charity, but we must also beware of seeing kitsch as a merely artistic deficiency, and art as a merely ornamental addition to life. We may answer that the morals and religion of these people are sound, and that the sentimental film may after all serve a good purpose. But in what way does it serve a good purpose? Alcohol promotes a feeling of well-being, it helps people to forget their worries and mistakes, it may make it easier for them to take decisions; but when the exhilaration passes off they have less strength and are more depressed than before. Because kitsch stupefies us it also deludes us as to its consequences.

The first of these is a slow, scarcely perceptible lowering of the whole level of religion and morality. If someone finds relaxation in kitsch, this is bound to begin to affect his whole life; secretly he begins to be content with the worthless and to take pleasure in it, he gives in to the untruthfulness of kitsch, and this will begin to be reflected in his behaviour; as kitsch forms of expression become acceptable, or at least familiar, at the periphery of his life, he will hardly be able to prevent them creeping also into his work, his preaching, teaching, the work of his hands. This must lower the quality of his output. And as we have seen, kitsch is a narcotic; as we become weaker we scarcely notice our decline. At the same time it gives the illusion of an experience of higher values, which, in a crisis, or as a motive for overcoming selfishness, will prove powerless.

The most disastrous effect of kitsch is necessarily on personal religious life. We have seen that kitsch tends to make use of higher values for its own ends. So long as these are within the hierarchy of creation there is no complete destruction of the values so misused; for all created things have the function of serving other values, even if they claim first of all to have a value in themselves. Even man himself may be made a means to an end, as long as his personal dignity is respected, as long as he is not *merely* serving as a means to an end.

But God, absolute and infinite, can never be used as a means to an end. If through kitsch we use God himself and our personal meeting with him to serve selfish ends, then we fail in our response to God. If we do this consciously and freely it involves grave moral fault. The true cult picture is a symbol through which the personal majesty and might of God is made present (as in the attitude to icons in the Eastern Church), but with religious kitsch there is no such experience of the divine presence. If we use the religious content of a picture as a means of personal satisfaction, we are overlooking the fact that in religion we confront, not a thing, but a person, one who speaks to us and demands our personal response. In kitsch, instead of meeting God we try to exploit him; our relationship is vitiated.

What is Kitsch?

In this description we have taken the effect of kitsch to its logical conclusion. Fortunately for most people this is much mitigated by some intention, in greater or less degree, to serve God and to seek his will. But is it really harmless that kitsch should be insinuating into our piety an attitude which of its nature excludes a religious meeting with God? Is it harmless if a "holy" picture is actually a false sign leading men, not to God, but to an idol, or to self-idolization? The enormous extent to which ordinary religious life has been affected in this way in the last hundred years presents a serious peril. Kitsch in word and picture has reduced God to a commodity for the purposes of spiritual pleasure; to what extent, for how many people, has this not prevented the experience of God's heart-touching, personal love and loving personality?

We have now reached the crux of our enquiry, the examination of kitsch in practical Christian life.

Part Two

KITSCH IN CATHOLIC WORSHIP
AND MORALITY

I

Kitsch in the Church Today

Liturgy

IN the Canon of the Mass, the administration of the sacraments, and the earliest evidences of the liturgical Christian life, there is as little of kitsch as in the Gospel itself. Here are religious actions and liturgical forms which emerged out of the most intense religious concentration and a conscious intention of obedience in the performance of holy rites; artistic considerations were not involved. Religious life was indeed expressed in visible forms, but it was that which the sign signified, the almost terrifyingly great supernatural event of salvation, which was absorbing, not the sign. The early Church had neither time nor interest in making the holy signs beautiful. Here at the heart of the liturgy and in its earliest forms, kitsch is absent, because its specific field, art, was not consciously considered and because no cheapness, self-indulgence, or pedantry could find a place in the austere and strict reverence for sacramental reality.

Nevertheless, the oldest forms of the liturgy and the first examples of visual religious art have a unique beauty in their austere simplicity. They were made by men of flesh and blood, and in giving a shape to that which they genuinely and seriously believed to be holy and good they spontaneously created beauty—in accordance with the laws of human and created nature, *bonum et pulchrum, sacrum et pulchrum convertuntur.*

It cannot be said that all the Church's liturgy is by its very nature protected against kitsch. Liturgy is the expression of life and is therefore subject to the laws of life; it sprouts, grows, blooms, fructifies, becomes rich in autumn colours, and can fade in its individual manifestations. In the later periods of liturgical development, liturgical prayer and action gained a wider range; there was leisure to embroider (for instance, the sequences in the Roman missal) and a deliberate attempt was made to find beautiful forms in word, picture and ceremony. Thus there was more scope for play, for enjoyment, and so an opening for kitsch; but though there is a certain artificiality in some of the Breviary hymns, liturgical prayer is too objective, too much the prayer of the Church, the action is too concentrated, for there to be time for indulgence in the pleasure of pious self-admiration.

Kitsch has to make its way in by devious routes; for instance, when in some way the liturgical action is deflected from its proper purpose, perhaps by the accompanying music. The Viennese orchestral Masses of the classical period are for the most part of the highest artistic quality, as well as the expression of personal devotion, but from the religious point of view they are rather a sharing through musical contact of private piety than a suitable accompaniment to the common Sacrifice of the Christian people. Later imitators of these composers therefore found the path to sugary devotion and kitsch prepared for them.

In the liturgy itself, the Church's rubrics are a safeguard; she imposes strict rules for the sacramental mysteries and makes these binding in conscience. On the liturgical periphery, however, she leaves considerable freedom and it is here that the kitsch of a particular period is able to establish itself, both for private devotion and popular forms of piety. The Church generously allows scope in

1. A Saint.
Carlo Dolci.

p. 6. A technically good painting can come perilously near to kitsch.

bunch of violets.
ürer.
lbertina, Vienna.

. 18, 22. A painting
n be religious in
eling without having
religious subject.

3. The Infant Jesus with St John and two angels. Rubens. *Kunsthisorisches Museum, Vienna.*

p. 39. A religious title to a painting does not necessarily make it a religious picture.

4. Jesus in the tabernacle.
Modern German drawing, by a woman.

pp. 40, 44. Trying to evoke a religious response by an emotional and disingenuous appeal.

5. The Gift of the Fear the Lord.
'Holy' card, printed Italy.

p. 40. Theological tru represented as trivial cosy.

6. The Christ of St John of the Cross.
Painting by Salvador Dali. *Glasgow Art Gallery and Museum.*

pp. 40, 154. A dramatic viewpoint and lighting used as a trick to catch
attention; realism used to make our Lord physically attractive.

7. The Sacrament of the Last Supper.
Painting by Salvador Dali. *National Gallery of Art, Washington, D.C. Chester Dale Collection.* pp. 41, 154. Centred on the effect to be produced on the spectator. The figures are arranged

8. The Rest on the Flight into Egypt. Painting by Philip Veit.

p. 42. A sincere religious painting; but the placid and idyllic atmosphere is remote from reality, and therefore paves the way to kitsch.

9. Mary as the Good Shepherdess. 'Holy' card, German.

p. 42. The bad qualities of Plate 8 without its redeeming sincerity and artistic talent; bogus in idea and feebly conventional in execution.

10. The Infant Samuel. Painting by Reynolds. *Tate Gallery, London.*

   pp. 43–4. A famous painting which has inspired kitsch art and kitsch reactions through its idealization of childhood innocence.

I offer You, dear Jesus,
   everything I do this day.

11. Baby Jesus. From a child's book printed in Italy.

   p. 44. God became a child for us, but the artist has turned him into a cuddly doll; a trashy, sentimental formula.

12. Our Lady.
Card printed in England.

pp. 46, 154. A drawing which purports to be our Lady, but the face and appeal are that of a film-star/pin-up girl.

e Penitent Magdalene.

Aesthetically this may be a good picture, but the erotic treatment of a subject 1 purports to be pious makes it kitsch.

14. The Light of the World.
Painting by Holman Hunt. *Keble College, Oxford.*

pp. 47, 110. A deeply religious painting by a great artist; but
there is a hiatus between the symbolism of the conception
and the realism of the representation.

15. Card of the Sacred Heart.   16a

Three typical German 'holy'-cards

16b   16c

pp. 48, 110, 146. The face in Plate 15 is a sentimentalized and debased version of a generalized type derived from old masters, completely lacking in any spiritual truth or reality. The artist has been responding not to personal feeling but to commercial demand. 16 *a*, *b* and *c* are traditional pious kitsch.

17a   17b

Madonna and Child. Two medals. Widely available.

p. 62. A modern type of
kitsch. The idea that it is
'modern' to be unrealistic
has been used as an excuse
for laziness. These are not
simplifications of form but
slurred drawing which is
meaningless and slovenly.

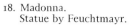

18. Madonna.
   Statue by Feuchtmayr.

   p. 71. Showing the rococo
   tendency to secularize
   religious subjects, a type
   of art which is liable to
   be experienced as kitsch.

19. Immaculata.
Statue by Günter.

20. Guardian angel.
Card printed in Italy.

p. 97. The Bible gives us descriptions of supernatural beings of power and majesty, this sort of representation reduces them to the sweet and wishy-washy.

21. Elijah, from Bible
illustrated by
Tissot (1902).
   p. 108. Lay figures,
badly drawn; the task
he set himself seems to
have been far beyond
the compass of the
artist's inspiration and
even his technical
gifts have failed him.

22. *Noli me tangere*,
from Bible illustrated
by Hole (1906).
   pp. 108, 149. Externals
of dress and setting
create a false verisimi-
litude which has de-
ceived people into be-
lieving that the reality
was like this; a com-
parison with Plate 24
demonstrates its banal
emptiness.

23. *Noli me tangere*.
Painting by
Graham Sutherland.
Chichester Cathedral.
   p. 109. A painting
where the artist has
been utterly involved
in his subject and has
put into each brush
stroke the intensity of
his own response.

Illustration by Jacques le Scanff from Joseph (Dove Books, 1966).

pp. 110, 152. Modern artists are using the direct approach of children's drawing as a means to circumvent the representational problems in religious art.

St Anthony.
Statue made in Italy.

pp. 97, 121, 132. A stereotyped idea of a sexless figure whose sanctity has been effortless.

26. Crucifixion.
Painting by Graham Sutherland. *Church of St. Aidan, East Acton.*

p. 134. A painting in which the artist has faced the subject as an encounte
tween God and ourselves as we are, in our world of indifference to him, of cru
and disillusion.

27. The Raising of Lazarus. Stained glass by John Piper, made by Patrick Reyntiens. *Eton College Chapel*, 1958.

p. 153. Successful modern use of symbolism.

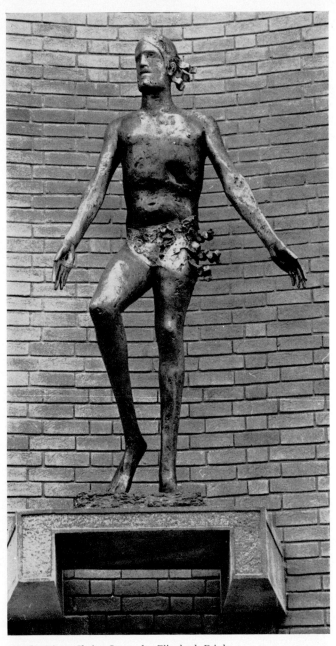

28. The Risen Christ. Statue by Elizabeth Frink.

p. 153. An example of creative religious art. The artist has been entirely committed to her vision of the reality and transcendence of her subject.

both the visual arts and church music for the activities of lesser minds and artists, and so too with an indulgent smile —far too indulgent?—she tolerates the dominion of kitsch in the very house of God, in order not to deter even unenlightened piety so long as it is in some degree genuine. In the last resort this genial tolerance implies a deep respect for the personal freedom of the Christian. Certain limits are of course imposed, for the sake of theological truth, moral purity and dignity, but wide scope is still left for kitsch.

Images of the Saints

Let us take a few typical examples. Kitsch appears in the imitation wood-carved crucifix, which is really plaster, or that which is plastic "imitation ivory", and in the imitation flowers, whether crudely coloured paper ones, or expensive and realistic wax or plastic.

Kitsch appears in the way in which stereotyped figures appear again and again. By all means let us have pictures and statues of our Lady of Lourdes, of the Little Flower, of St Anthony holding the Christ Child (Plate 25), the sad thing is that it is always the same type for each of these saints. It is not merely that this is cheap in the material sense, but that it is also kitsch in the sense that an easy way has been taken to avoid the effort and courage required to deal with anything unique.

Kitsch appears also in the sweetening and prettifying of sacred figures. Let us consider first the usual modern representation of an angel. In the biblical descriptions of angelic appearances, both in the New Testament and the Old, the impression given is of beings of more than earthly majesty and power. "His appearance was like lightning, and his raiment white as snow. And for fear of him the guards trembled and became like dead men. But the angel said to the women, 'Do not be afraid'" (Matt. 28.3-5). What is there in Scripture that gives us the right to evoke these spirits of terrible might as the familiar wishy-washy guardian angel representation (Plate 20)? There is of course a difficulty in that angels are sexless. But in the Bible they appear in the form of young men (Mark. 16.5 Acts 1.10), not as impotent hermaphrodites. Then there is the question of the merry, rosy, naked cherubs; are we justified in so depicting these blessed spirits who always see the face of the Father? (Matt. 18.10.) On rococo altars the crescendo of cherubs does indeed symbolize and suggest the spontaneous, joyous assent of creation to the Creator, and they are not thought of, at least by the initiated, as angels in the proper sense of the word. But the debased twee versions of these figures (Plate 20) have reduced the ordinary Christian's idea of an angel to kitsch particularly because this is the picture so often offered to him in childhood. Even so it is perhaps less harmful than the insipid "grown-up" angel.

Our saints meet the same fate. In Gothic paintings and manuscripts they were often represented against a background of gold or abstract pattern, symbolizing the timelessness and unalterable validity of their holiness. The ideal background supplied in modern kitsch pictures has a different connotation; the saints appear to be raised above the ugly realities of this world, and the struggle with sin and the consequences of sin. Yet all the saints, with the exception of our Lady, had to wrestle with sin, and were marked by sin, and even she knew the universal consequences of sin, age, pain and want. Kitsch pictures and statues of saints, however, invariably show them in a sort of Christian Arcadia, and to judge from these it would appear that becoming a saint is a gentle, pleasant, but rather boring process. All this is bound to dull the perception of those who regularly pray before such statues.

Up to a point kitsch is relative; things can be tolerated in secular life, even in private devotion, which are not fit for public worship. The nearer kitsch is allowed to approach to the central Mystery of Christian worship the more repulsive it is and the more disastrous. At least we do not need to go and look at the Lourdes Grotto theatrically lit with coloured lights if it is in some obscure corner of the church, but the sentimental figure of Mary on the back of a chasuble, or above the altar, is unavoidable, and the person sensitive to true values will be repelled, and the more repelled the more real his love of our Lady.

Popular Hymns

A hymn is a poem or verse set to music; there can be kitsch in the words, or the music, or the way in which the words are adapted to the music, or the way in which the hymn is sung—as we have already seen (p. 52). The Catholic tradition of Latin hymns is superb, *Christus vincit*, *Ave Maris Stella*, *Te Joseph celebrent*, for instance. But even here a difficulty arises; in translation unfortunately a wonderful hymn can easily be kitsch, particularly a translation from Latin into English, where the essential conciseness and terse antitheses of the original are almost impossible to render. The nineteenth-century habit of flowery devotional language, derived from a weakened strain of the ecstatic vein native to the seventeenth century, usually in fact puts a complete barrier between us and the original poem.

To turn first to kitsch in hymn verses, and the sentiments, theological and otherwise, which they express:

99

here are two verses from the hymn to the Sacred Heart "To Jesus' Heart all burning":

> As thou art meek and lowly
> And ever pure of heart,
> So may my heart be wholly
> Of thine the counterpart.
>
> When life away is flying,
> And earth's false glare is done;
> Still, Sacred Heart, in dying
> I'll say I'm all thine own.

The first verse is an insult to the Redeemer, and the second casts a slur upon his creation. In what way can my heart be a counterpart to God's? The words conjure up a picture of two beings equally innocuous and unreal, the atmosphere evoked is completely remote from the tensions of Christian life, and conveys just that false idea of painless piety and easy despising of the world to which we shall have to return.

In the Breviary there are hymns to our Lady which make appeal to all that a man who is a Christian can wish to express to show his devotion to the Mother of God. The writers of these hymns found words which are manly which we admire, and which we can make our own as we sing them. But, alas! we are often asked instead to make a very different approach to our Lady. When we are invited to sing a hymn which opens with the words,

> This is the image of our Queen,

any man of imagination might conjure up some memory of a Madonna like the Black Virgin of Monserrat. But no such vision of objective reality will be left for him to contemplate by the time he has reached the following fiction;

> Sweet are the flow'rets we have culled,
> This image to adorn;
> But sweeter far is Mary's self,
> That rose without a thorn.

He will in fact most probably find himself thinking not of our Lady, but of one of those statues described on p. 77, with painted plaster roses at its feet.

Our Lord and our Lady have fared badly at the hands of the writers of hymns in English. The saints have fared even worse. Kitsch runs riot and insult is added to insult as verse succeeds verse in hymns "devoted" to Saints Joseph, Benedict, Patrick, David, Winifred—to say nothing of my Guardian Angel. Take, for instance, the following hymn to St George:

> The land of my love is a desert,
> Its temples and altars are bare,
> The finger of death is upon it,
> The footprints of Satan are there.

The picture is so overdrawn that it is quite unreal. A shining exception are Cardinal Newman's hymn to St Michael, "Thou champion high" (written possibly before his conversion), and the translation of the vesper hymn to SS. Joachim and Anne, "Blest is the holy Joachim".

If we turn now to music, many of our worst hymn tunes are fortunately being replaced with worthier models, notably since the new liturgy for Low Mass has come into being. And yet kitsch is hard of dying. A crop of the hoariest examples may be found in the Appendix to the New Westminster Hymnal. The selection of "alternative tunes" printed there provides an excellent source for the study of kitsch in this field. Comparing these with the settings by composers of, say, the period of Gibbons, we recognize in the melodies of that earlier period a smoothness of rise and fall which invites the voice to respond to the eloquence of musical line. By contrast our recent specimens resemble ladders from which several rungs have been maliciously removed; the music sounds a chord and then the voice is made to sing an arpeggio on that chord as if the human voice were a bugle. The impoverishment becomes manifest, and is clear in such examples as "Jesus my Lord", "Immaculate Mary", "Daily, daily", "Faith of our fathers", "Arm, arm for the struggle approaches".

Amongst the composers who figure in the Appendix we find Mr Hemy. In fairness let it be said that the melodies from his pen have a certain radiance which those of the hymns just quoted cannot emulate. The temptation is to saddle these melodies with harmonies which are immediately recognizable as kitsch to any musician. Cloying chromatics coupled with an unsingable arpeggio vitiate that (happily anonymous) hymn to the Sacred Heart, "To Jesus' Heart all burning". The chromatics occur on "Heart all", and the arpeggio is the bugle-call for the word "burning". In the next verse the arpeggio becomes unsingable because the text is "O Heart, for me on fire" . . . and no congregation will effect any other articulation of this last word than Faa-ee-yur. How can they help it? The workmanship is bad. Unfortunately people "like" the tune, and we are usually told that they should be allowed to sing what they like. The answer is surely that they should be told to consider truthfully why they like it: is it that they sing for the glory of God, or for their own mixed-motive pleasure? Hymns such as this might profitably be compared with "And though the Seraphim above", or "Come, Holy Ghost, creating fire".

Devotional Articles

If our Lord were to come again and journey to one of the modern pilgrimage centres of Europe, instead of to the Temple of Jerusalem, would he look at the piety stalls round the shrine and their goods and say, "Suffer the little children to come unto me and forbid them not", or would he seize a whip and overturn the tables? Pious pilgrims buy the figures for sale in such stalls and shops; they are hung up in the houses of Catholic families and children are taught to pray before them: the more simple the person is, the more he will identify the image with the reality; imperceptibly the image builds up the idea of Christ in his mind. But this cheap plaster or plastic cast of the well-shaped body of a "handsome man" who seems to come to the Cross so casually and painlessly, has this image really anything to do with the Lord who died for us? If we give these to children, are we really bringing them to Christ, or are we actually doing our best to prevent them from knowing him as he really is?

The crude impropriety of the picture of St Joseph on a beer-mug, of saints on ash-trays, of clockwork statues of the Pope which can be wound up to give a blessing, is unmistakable. But there are also the sweet and attractive holy pictures which go into the pilgrim's prayer book, and it is not only in some pilgrimage centres that these things are sold, but in the well-ordered shops of our cities and towns, in Catholic repositories everywhere, and even at the doors of our churches.

Kitsch in Catholic Worship and Morality

"Edifying" Literature

There is a short period in the development of a child when it is only just beginning to discover moral values and can only grasp these in a simplified presentation. Very soon such edifying simplifications cease to convince, and begin in fact to have the opposite effect. In the same way hagiography which offers us a history of girlhood innocence divorced from all compromising situations and all possible temptations, is kitsch, because it represents the virtue of purity as something cosy and obvious. It may provide enjoyable reading, but if the pleasure is in something which claims to express the wholeness of life when it does no such thing, then the pleasure will have been in kitsch. False zeal can only cause damage, and this holds also for unenlightened pastoral zeal which is applied to writing "useful" stories for calendars and magazines. As we have seen, art which is used as a means to an end is bound to be kitsch. Shortsighted expediency, cheap content, and carelessness in literary form, can all create kitsch in writing.

Kitsch and the Priest

This is a theme which we must discuss with great tact. Every sentence could be regarded as presumptuous criticism and pedantry. We only want to look at the facts, not to hurt anybody. What we have to say will take the form of a warning about possibilities, rather than an attack on existing abuses. Because the priest has taken on such an overwhelmingly sacred task, he can never be too sensitive to the slightest trace of kitsch in the exercise of his functions. It is not easy for the ordinary man to distinguish between the minister and his office, the symbol and what is symbolized. Kitsch seen in the priest will cast its shadow over his idea of religion and of the Church. Even more disastrous may be the effect of a priest's uncritical acceptance of kitsch in his manner and behaviour. Kitsch is infectious; seen in the life of the pastor, it imperceptibly begins to colour the life of the parish, or at least of its keenest members.

In the first place there is the way in which the presbytery is furnished. There has never been a parish priest who put up with a house full of kitsch side by side with a church which was dignified and beautiful.

We are here, however, mainly concerned with kitsch in priestly functions. The unctuous or emotional sermon is kitsch. The preacher who is really zealous for souls will avoid all deliberately sweet, flowery language; he will also refrain from the accusing cries of a moralizing Cassandra over abandoned youth, and from the jargon of the streets which is sometimes used by the preacher who wishes to prove his knowledge of the world. The priest has to preach God and his saving deeds; if his sermon is kitsch, it is himself, not God, whom he presents for the admiration of his parishioners.

Kitsch in preaching is deplorable; at the sick-bed it looks much uglier. The priest who enjoys playing the part of the Good Shepherd, and the warmth of his own feeling, brings no comfort to the sick. Kitsch can also glide into the confessional. How great is the temptation for some priests to feel at home as benign spiritual fathers (or jovial-pious spiritual uncles), and so send their penitents from the confessional relieved and touched by this kind understanding man, but without clear resolutions or a soul transformed.

All this is still a question of the word of the priest addressed to men. But what shall we say of the priest who, when he kneels before the altar as consecrated repre-

sentative of his people and prays to the living God, does so
sentimentally? He speaks to God and yet in the emotional
tone of his voice, in his ostentatiously folded hands, and
in his deep-bowed head, he reveals his own vanity. It may
be that some Christian, fully aware of the grandeur of the
Mass, is approaching the table of the Lord with humility
and reverence; but he is torn from his devotion by the
unctuous sentimentality of the minister as he gives holy
communion. He becomes aware that the priest is capable
of exploiting even this occasion to indulge in a theatrical
performance.

The reader will pardon us for insisting on this point. It
is important to see how serious moral defects may be concealed behind that which seems to be merely tasteless.
Slight and scarcely noticed openings for kitsch present a
danger just because they are relatively harmless; while
some people become accustomed and indifferent to them,
others, already mistrustful or hostile to the Church, are
confirmed in their attitude.

II

Art and Kitsch in Religion

True Religious Art

WE have tried to enumerate the fields of Catholic life where kitsch has found its widest scope and where it is the greatest danger. Now we have to interpret these facts and to see their bearing upon religious art as such, and the ideal of Christian living. We have considered art and kitsch, and its disintegrating moral effects; we need now to approach the problem from the more positive angle of true religious art, and its place in Christian life.

How does a work that is specifically religious art—not just art—come into being? The essential condition must be a corresponding religious experience in the mind of the artist. Normally this leads to his choosing a religious subject, or alternatively the subject may arouse the experience. All creation, however, reflects its Creator, and a secular subject may therefore kindle a religious experience in a religious person and produce a religious effect. The poetry of Gerard Manley Hopkins is an example; almost every poem, whatever the subject, is a religious poem. Indeed, in a sense every true work of art is religious, since it brings to the beholder a peace that is not of this world, and presents an eschatological promise and an inkling of the "new earth" to come.

Lack of Religious Inspiration

But this is true only in general; just as a secular subject

may inspire a religious work of art, so a religious subject offers no guarantee of a resulting religious work, still less of a work suitable for cult purposes: and this may be the case even when there is no reason to doubt the artist's faith and sincerity. We have already come across this possibility when discussing rococo statues. Later examples are found in the biblical illustrations of Tissot, which have unfortunately had a very wide influence; they became the prototype of a school of debased illustration, best known in the work of William Hole, which is still widely current in Catholic as well as Protestant works. Tissot's work is certainly sincere and he was an accomplished painter whose pictures of the social scene in London and Paris are delightful. What is wrong in Plate 21 ? Possibly the artist had no genuine religious experience *as an artist*; he certainly lacked the vitality and spiritual force to express such experience visually. Tissot went himself to the Holy Land as a preparation for the work of biblical illustration which he set himself; but he found there nothing but externals. There is no sense of a real historic happening in this painting, instead we see the theatrical posing of two figures. Still less is there any sense of supernatural power in the figure of Elijah, or of the drama of the moment, of the parched land and "the little cloud like a man's hand" appearing in answer to his prayer. Instead there is only the sentimental trick of the setting sun. Sadly enough, even Tissot's technical ability seems to have left him when he set himself this task which was beyond his capacity, the paintings are badly composed and shoddy in drawing. In these aspects the work of Hole is weaker still. He too went to Palestine, and the pernicious thing about his work is that to those who are not used to making aesthetic judgments, his illustrations give the impression of reality—the externals are here, clothes, surroundings, trappings all giving verisimilitude to the idea that it would have looked like this had we been there. But could that momentous meeting on Easter morning have looked banal like this? (Plate 22). The Magdalene looks as if she were doing some pious exercise, while our Lord is a wishy-washy lay-figure in white draperies; these are not even real people meeting. Let us look instead at the Graham Sutherland painting at Chichester (Plate 23); here surely is an expression of the tremendous emotional impact of that meeting; the very awkwardness of her contorted pose conveys the reality of the reaction of Mary Magdalene the sinner to this new and overwhelming presence of the risen Lord, part stranger, part lover, newly met in a unique moment.

Types of Art and Types of Response

For Tissot and Hole the fault lay partly perhaps in the spirit of the age in which they lived. Other artists of the nineteenth century, Dyce, Holman Hunt, and Millais, painted religious pictures which are in a completely different category, with far greater imaginative depth and technical brilliance; all the same something is wrong, as we have seen also in the German Nazarenes (p. 42). There are times when conditions seem to be lacking for that intensive grasp and understanding of the Christian message which is necessary before this can find expression in the symbol of artistic form. This seems to have been the case in the nineteenth century, the "century without grace", which, even in Catholic theology, rediscovered only in its second half the unique character of grace and its relationship to human nature. An artist might be quite sensitive to religious values and possess the gifts necessary to express them, but the world in which he lived was too anthropocentric, the human element in the representation of a religious subject, the historical background, the "shell of private individual experience" was too strong even in a symbolically conceived painting like *The Light of the World* (see p. 47) for him to be able to achieve great religious art. One of the signs of this weakness was the tendency to adopt the canons of beauty belonging to an earlier period. In Germany the return to the pre-baroque tradition of Raphael produced an insipid classicism which, as we have seen (p. 73), eventually produced one of the worst types of kitsch from the importation of which we suffer (as in Plate 15). In England we have had various stages of a revival of medieval forms. In both cases, the artists have been unable to breathe spiritual or human life into the shapes of the past. In an age in which men live stunted lives the artistic powers necessary to evoke the whole man—that is man as open to grace—are likely to be lacking. The way to kitsch must then be short.

Religious art must embody a religious experience which is real in both the aesthetic and the spiritual sphere. It also, like every other work of art, requires technical skill. The infantilism, real or adopted, to which some Catholic artists have turned today (Plate 24) in the present stylistic dilemma seems a way out which, at this late stage in the history of culture, may lead very quickly to kitsch. Nor is technique enough in itself. Like every other work of art a religious work must be the expression of the inner transformation of the subject into something of universal validity through the medium of the artist's unique, individual style of expression; particularly must this be so in a religious work, since without this personal commitment what appears to sense can never be transformed into a sacramental symbol.

The response to religious art is also a challenge. Again, a secular subject may be experienced in a truly religious way where the beholder is a truly religious person for whom all creation is transparent. There is also the fact that art—it has been explicitly asserted for music, but holds also to a lesser extent for painting and sculpture—gives sensible expression to a whole range of our emotional and spiritual capacities; to kindness towards others, and readiness to help, to enthusiasm, to repulsion and so on. When these—for instance, in a Beethoven symphony—find a powerful and compelling expression, the listener will be enthralled; but he will probably not grasp the objective content which this expression signified to the composer, what he thought, or what ideas influenced him while he composed. Every hearer will have to draw from his own immediate environment his interpretation of the content and motive force which lie behind the movements of comfort, defiance, enthusiasm, which the music excites within him. For one hearer devotion will take on romantic associations, for another religious, for another political or social colour, for each according to his temperament. Thus some of the finest pieces of folk music have at different periods been given both secular and religious words (Bach, for instance, used the folk song *Innsbruck ich muss dich lassen* in his St Matthew Passion).

In art which is directly religious, however, the unbiased listener or beholder is not roused to any analogous feeling or reaction, but is directly addressed as a religious person; herein lies the uplifting and invigorating power of genuine religious art. But it must be genuine; the result of a real and intense experience. If the artist is guilty of self-deception, of misusing his subject as a pretext beneath which he is actually presenting some different feeling, erotic perhaps or self-comforting, then the beholder will be confused. He will find that he is not drawn to prayer; on the contrary, he finds himself moved in a way which corresponds to some other instinct evoking sensuous, merely pleasurable response. This fact of course demonstrates the infectiousness of kitsch.

We are again brought up against the truth that the decisive factor in the production of a religious work of art is the experience of the artist, that this is communicated, and that the response to it is a dialogue with the artist. It is as if someone came to a strange town, guidebook in hand. Alone he will find it difficult to feel its life and appreciate its beauty, but if a friend who is native to the town comes with him and imparts his own love of its beauty and his own sense of its life, then the experience of the stranger will be immensely enhanced; it will be an experience of the town, and at the same time of the image of the town in the mind of his friend. In the same way religious art can both introduce us to religion, and clarify and intensify it in a way which would be impossible for us to achieve alone. By a typically human process we help one another. And where, in his metaphysical foolishness, is modern man more alone, and more in need of help, than in religion?

A Summary

To sum up, there seem to be five categories of religious art; there are illustrations of religious subjects which are not yet art and therefore cannot be kitsch. If an eye is placed diagrammatically in a triangle we have a generally understood symbol of the triune God. It is an aid to understanding, but the form as such does not demand any response, because it does not involve any artistic intention.

At the opposite pole is the genuinely religious work; a religious subject or one related to religion, which has been given a form both religious and artistic.

Thirdly, we have genuine, even sublime works representing a religious subject, but not inspired by religious experience. Here again is no question of kitsch.

Fourthly, the work may be lacking in aesthetic quality, either because it is artistically inadequate, merely realistic, or because it is a kitsch work making use of a religious subject.

Finally, there is kitsch religious art, work which is not altogether lacking either in religious inspiration or in artistic quality, but in which there is some bogus element of frivolity or sentimentality which invites a kitsch response.

Response to religious art can be similarly summarized. We can experience as kitsch that which is really kitsch (although its subject may be religious); that which is religious with elements of kitsch; and that which is true and genuine religious art. In all these cases the man who experiences the kitsch is wholly or in part to blame.

Secondly, the response can be mixed, partly a genuine artistic response, partly kitsch, either derived from the work, or supplied by the viewer.

Thirdly, there may be a genuine religious experience— not aesthetic—from a work which is in fact kitsch, but which has a religious subject. This happens with educated as well as simple people and explains how upright and highly moral people come to prefer kitsch religious art. Actually it is not a real preference for kitsch, but a strong and spontaneous reaction to the recognizable and realistic representation of the subject (at which kitsch artists are often particularly successful), which by-passes the morally and artistically worthless experience which lies behind the actual representation. All the same, it is hard to understand how such people can remain permanently blind to the spurious image which is still—even if only semi-

H   113

consciously tolerated—a part of the content of their experience.

Fourthly, there may be a purely aesthetic experience of a religious work of art; this occurs when the viewer is wholly uninterested in religion.

The final and solely desirable response is that of an experience both truly religious and truly aesthetic, to a true work of art which is also truly religious.

Kitsch as a Danger to Religion

There can be kitsch in any sort of art, but religion of its nature offers particularly advantageous openings. Devotion is concerned with the most exalted objects; it is governed and roused by truths made known to man through revelation and handed down with the greatest reverence from generation to generation. It is natural to extend this reverence also to the outward forms of religious life. Even when these have kitsch characteristics, we preserve them despite their artistic (and moral) worthlessness. We do not dare to throw away the plaster crucifix which belonged to our parents; they were fond of it, and moreover it is the figure of our Lord.

This mistaken extension of piety means not only that we continue to keep in use kitsch representations, but also that we maintain infantile conceptions. The things which we keep are often things given to us as children, suitable as means for making religious truth perceptible to the child but in the meantime our knowledge of religion has grown and now needs to be given forms corresponding to a more mature experience of life. Too often this does not happen the stereotyped images and clichés which we learnt at convent school or in religious instruction, which were simplified and emotionally determined, and often turned into kitsch, for the child, are not replaced; the unkind expression "suitable for nuns" is unfortunately not always altogether unjustified. Even if what we were given was not actually kitsch, it tends to become so to adults, because it does not correspond to adult experience. This reacts upon religion itself, which becomes tedious because it has not been separated from the childish presentation which is no longer viable. Lack of thought and piety often enter into a strange marriage; kitsch is the fruit of the union.

Art is not absolutely necessary to religious life. If need be, piety can make do with any kind of sensible sign, without considering the task of giving it artistic form, and therefore without touching the field of the beautiful. Nevertheless, such a situation can only be temporary and is certainly not ideal. Art has its place in religion, it is its function to glorify God by giving to piety an appropriate outward expression. Religion practised without this normal human adjunct is primitive and crude. It is, moreover, dangerous. It is often held that from the pastoral point of view it is completely irrelevant whether people are edified by a great work of art or by something artistically insignificant. This is false; partly because it denies art its function in religion, partly because an experience of the holy derived from a work of art, but not through its artistic quality (as described on pp. 113-51), has a less enduring effect on the soul, and through its isolation from artistic values opens the way to kitsch. The more one-sided and exclusive a person's devotion to religion is, the greater is his danger from this source.

This sounds a paradoxical statement, for who, in principle, should be further from the pace-makers of kitsch, from the characteristics of hypocrisy, sloth and pleasure-seeking than the morally energetic and truly devout Christian? The answer is that if we consider aesthetic values as unimportant or try to replace them with moral and religious values, considering these to be higher, we are trying to cut out part of the meaning of life; we cannot do this with impunity. Moral and religious values do not reveal themselves to men with their full urgency unless clothed in beauty. Beauty lights up the good and the holy, but it also has laws proper to itself. People whose moral-religious outlook is narrow and restricted think that these laws can be disregarded; at the same time, they know that the spiritual sense of the holy can only be grasped if it is given some visible or audible form, and so they look for some sort of forcible expression. So the noisy speech of kitsch seems useful. They forget that, as Goethe has told us, "an intimation of the morally sublime can only be expressed through art, and that in art the only way in which this can be embodied is a way which is sensuously sublime".

The kitsch which is unconsciously employed in the ways which we have been considering may be preferred out of naïve sentimentality, but it may also easily be the more harmful, dishonest type which, itself originating in unclean and dishonest intentions, falsifies the moral and religious content which it purports to express.

When this happens, it is not a tragedy but a sin. Such people no doubt fight shy of open sensuality, but they commit the sin of secret pride, forgetting that they are dependent on the body and its senses, and despising the artistic values which are linked to these. Such pious folk do not want to be moral and religious as human beings, but as incorporeal spirits. By running away from beauty and not troubling about the artistic clothing of the good and holy, they free themselves from the ties of true, sensible beauty, only to fall into the slavery of sensually deceptive kitsch. It is the typical temptation of the ascetic.

We can get the same deplorable result if art is not ignored, but used only as a means; when it is recognized as related to what is holy, but in such a subordinated way that reverence for God leads to neglect of reverence for art, and its intrinsic value is ignored. So we get the pious hymns which are judged only according to their pastoral-pedagogic usefulness (see pp. 99, 88). A hymn is not just an expression of piety; it must be taken seriously first of all as song, as a form of beauty, to be beautifully sung; only so can it arouse the appropriate response of reverence and joy. So it will also best serve pastoral aims.

If, on the other hand, the aesthetic function is by-passed, the sensible element in the hymn, which ought to lead us through its artistic form into the realm of the spirit, will not be effective as a symbol, because this link—the artistic form—will be inadequate. Religion will not be effectively linked to the sensible and so the latter will demand experience for its own sake. So we shall fall into religious kitsch, and the hymn will fail both as art and as religion.

Even apart from such misunderstanding of the function of beauty in the sphere of religion, there is a temptation to kitsch in the very fact that religious experiences are so deeply penetrating, and at their most sublime, in mystical contemplation, so remote from sense. Here below we do not see God, we have constantly to remind ourselves of his reality in earthly symbols. So the symbol is apt to become over important until it altogether overshadows that which is symbolized. In particular, in representations of the life of our Lord, the human circumstances are apt to overshadow the significance of the event in redemptive history; in work such as Plate 22, one feels that this has not entered into the artist's conception. By emphasizing the symbol, the thing symbolized has almost melted away. Again, because of the remoteness from sense of its reality, joy in religion does not easily enter into our consciousness, and even by God's design it may often be withheld from the Christian striving for perfection. Ascetical theology speaks of spiritual dryness, comfortlessness, and mystical theology of the dark night of sense. Profane art is near to everyday experience and to physical life, and true response to its theme is not so demanding as it is in the religious sphere. Because of this remoteness, religious experience may tend to be replaced by joy in the human or in the sensual content of the work of art; and so kitsch is able to impose itself on religious life and debase it. In the field of religious experience, there is thus always a danger of giving way to kitsch instead of facing an experience which brings out the "remoteness" of God. In so far as recent religious life has been orientated away from its sacramental core towards an anthropocentric emphasis this danger has grown.

Happiness in the realm of the holy is essentially something promised, which lies in the future. We cannot on our own initiative realize it at present, and we ought therefore not to waste our efforts in trying to do so. The danger then exists of a pseudo-interest and a pseudo-hope in the religious sphere. Who is there who does not occasionally catch himself out, sometimes longing for heaven, at other times pretending to himself that he possesses an inner independence of "this world", just because something has gone wrong with his mundane affairs? Instead of enduring the earthly disappointment and pain in the sphere in which it is experienced, we take refuge in a dream, in a pseudo-religious makeshift satisfaction. It costs nothing to hope for heaven when we have just experienced "how wicked this world is". To do this also makes us seem devout and aloof from the world. We treat religion as a refuge for our inferiority, for our incapacity to face up to life here and now, and our unwillingness to make a real sacrifice of the higher worldly values.

Charles Péguy lashed this attitude in the following words: "Because they lack the power (and the grace) to belong to nature, they think already that they belong to grace. Because they do not possess the courage of this world, they think that they have penetrated to the depths of eternity. Because they have not the courage to take sides among men, they think that they are already on God's side . . . because they love nobody they think that they love God." Such pseudo-religious cowardice engenders and nourishes much of the worst and most stubborn types of kitsch.

III

The Kitsch Ideal of the Christian Man

WHETHER it is the cause or the effect of atrophy in religion, kitsch is always a scandal which contributes to a further breakdown of Christian life.

In the history of the kitsch of the last hundred years, there is unconsciously exposed the unhappy effects of modern individualism by which the true picture of the Christian man and the abundantly rich life which Christ brought to us has been replaced by a caricature. The results are disastrous either way; an acceptance of the caricature as an ideal leads to the death of Christian life, and a rejection leads to the rejection with it of the reality which it misrepresents.

The model for this false picture of Christian life derives in Germany from the middle-class man of the turn of the century, a type already culturally and religiously degenerate, who has now been largely banished from public life as a result of the upheavals of our time. His outlook on life, however, still persists in this its last refuge, the religious sphere. In countries which have not suffered such devastating experiences he is perhaps not quite so obsolete. The picture is of a well-sheltered man who does not need to worry or to exert himself; one who is in fact inert and unperturbed, for ever remote from the realities of life.

Those who accept this picture are thereby refusing to recognize the disturbing and burdensome tensions of the

Christian life, particularly the tension between nature and super-nature. The anthropology of these pious pictures, narratives and plays reflects the attitude which is known theologically as Deism. Supernatural reality is not indeed denied; it is in fact disregarded. The saints of these pictures betray no hint of a natural existence threatened by the abyss of sin and endangered by "the mystery of iniquity" (2 Thess. 2.7). They give us no inkling of the real men who were able to pass over the abyss of hell only by way of the bridge of the Cross, who were in their lifetime marked by the pain of that Cross.

The kitsch saint is a relatively inoffensive man (Plate 25). The pain and care of his historical life are only related or depicted in the narrative or the image, not evoked in their asphyxiating power. There are types of crucifixes and martyrdom scenes in which the peaceful figures appear to be schizophrenic, able to smile in the midst of the most cruel agony, because suffering and pain have been split off in them.

There is also lacking that deeper grief of man in that he has to work out his salvation in fear and trembling (Phil. 2. 12). In the world of religious kitsch, man is not attacked by temptation. Goodness triumphs without ever having risked defeat, and consequently without the jubilation of having escaped damnation, without the joy of being redeemed.

Kitsch art represents the semi-Christian or unchristian attitude which is concerned with security at all costs. These saints relieve us of any anxiety about their reliability; the very possibility of sin is remote from them. And for this reason of course they have also had no need of God's mercy. And here lies the most serious of the charges against kitsch; it is a fundamental deception about the message of salvation; it leads us to forget that humanity needed to be saved, and in so doing it makes the Cross of our Lord unintelligible and superfluous.

The picture of the Christian man presented by kitsch—and we are thinking now of the pious man in the pictures, rather than the saints—lacks any suggestion of the tension of our situation within redemptive history. In the New Testament we constantly come across the tension in the life of the Christian who is sacramentally already dead and risen with Christ (Rom. 6. 2), and at the same time passionately straining forward to what lies ahead (Phil. 3. 13). Instead of this the kitsch figures appear in an anticipated transfiguration. These are not people who have been left, by the will of Christ, still in the world (John 17. 15), to stand against the stream, and bear him witness even in the face of death. Dynamism is lacking, for these people are enjoying the peace that Christ did not bring. That peace which radiates through hurts and necessities endured, which is the fruit of self-forgetting and strenuous faith, hope and charity, of this they convey no hint.

Does the guilt of kitsch which travesties our faith lie solely with the generation which has given it its immense success, or is it a question of the sins of the fathers becoming visible and being punished in the third, fourth, or even the tenth generation? One wonders whether the inadequate representation of Christian man, dull, spineless, self-satisfied, incapable of either the depths or the heights of Christian experience, is not connected with the post-Renaissance representations of our Lord, where a sense of his divinity has been more and more lost behind the picture of his handsome humanity. And here certainly the tradition goes back to the great masters, Raphael, Titian, Rubens; it is a hard saying, but religious kitsch is their illegitimate successor.

What is the moral image of man presented in pious

kitsch? In the Middle Ages the whole sphere of human experience was seen to be governed by the cardinal virtues and their interplay in the soul. In kitsch not only has the tension between body and soul, of which original sin makes us so painfully aware, disappeared, but also the differentiation in virtue. The same expressionless sugary figure serves as a symbol for fortitude or purity or humility. We can no longer recognize virtue as Aquinas described it, as *ultimum potentiae*, that is, the loveliest and richest upsurge of the life of an alert mind and a determined will. We are no longer stirred by religious art to brace ourselves, to rouse ourselves to effort and emulation. It inculcates instead the feeling that being devout means that kind of peaceful worthiness which sits out our earthly time and waits for heaven.

For this undisturbed repose in what purports to be a religious ideal a price has to be paid, which, if it does not destroy man, beggars him spiritually. It ignores another fundamental tension, that between the general human condition and the uniqueness of the person; not only are all the different saints made to look the same, but our churches are full of actual replicas. Here religious kitsch smooths the way for the propaganda which seeks to reduce the unique person to the collective mass-man.

There is yet another important reason for the absence of a natural human dynamism in religious kitsch; it reduces the difference between the sexes to a minimum. One gets the impression of impotence. At the time when religious kitsch had its greatest proliferation, in the last century, chastity was seen to be the most important of the virtues, and charity was forced into the background. Kitsch shows how far real chastity was then misunderstood; it was no longer regarded as a peak attained in the mastery of full-blooded human sexuality by the strength

123

of love and intelligence, but was turned into a diminution of humanity, an aversion from sex, mere repression. Chastity comes to mean knowing as little as possible about sex, having no interest in it, and practically no temptations. This ideal is strikingly expressed in pious kitsch. This is not only a travesty of sanctity, but, as we have already seen (p. 78), opens the door to pious sensuality; it all seems so upright and sexless that it is easy to abandon ourselves to softly-sweet piety, which may really be the expression of quite different subconscious urges. Moreover, this attempted de-sexualizing of man leaves no room for the true Eros, that mental-emotional-sensual force which draws man out of himself and compels him to encounter another person in his whole being. True religious feeling and Eros cannot be separated; when the natural emergence of love between the sexes is not experienced as a concrete reality, religious feeling may easily degenerate into a kind of moralistic deism and the experience of immediate personal encounter with God also be lost.

The picture of the good Christian in kitsch is characteristically inoffensive, and his background is made to match. The children of God enjoy their Sabbath rest and are content with their gifts. In kitsch this idea of "child" is not that of the mature man reborn, but instead a transference of the characteristics of biological infancy to the adult. The gentle melancholy of the Victorian idea of earthly childhood—a transition, a short span of blessed innocence—provides a tempting form for sentimental kitsch, particularly if the idea is associated with a happy Catholic childhood. Thus the devout Christian quite often sees the child of God as an adult projected back into an artificial childhood, and so, since we are children, it is natural to let others take care of us, to make a show of helplessness. In convents there is often an excessive importance attached to obedience and to a virginity not grasped in real depth; an affected childishness in regard to the reverend mother is then extended to religious forms of expression. These in turn affect the pupils and become a prolific source of pious kitsch.

How far is the prevalence of kitsch due to the fact that women are in the majority among practising Catholics, and that the market for kitsch, apart from the clergy, is largely feminine? It is difficult to distinguish cause and effect. Has kitsch tended to drive men out of the Church, or has it appeared because of their absence? Both factors may have been influential. In any case, the image of man which lies behind kitsch products seems to be a feminine ideal, which links up also with a feminine stress on "baby Jesus" which is so prevalent in Catholic books for children.

Part Three

OVERCOMING KITSCH

I

The Aesthetic Approach

LIKE the rest of man's failings, kitsch is with us till the Lord returns to establish a "new earth and a new heaven". But this sober observation must not lead us to accept this situation. The amount of kitsch in Christian life is not a matter of indifference; at the very least we must do something to arrest it. Some people have demanded compulsory measures to abolish it and to control the sale of devotional articles. This seems unwise. The positive step of trying to promote good religious art which shall be generally available is a much better alternative. A desirable move which has been suggested is that some mark of quality should be given to recommended devotional articles, and that episcopal commissions might also assist producers with advice. The real task, however, is to help the individual Catholic to see kitsch for what it is, to face up to his real reasons for liking it. This is an educational and pastoral duty which can be faced in several ways.

In the light of Christian ethics art is not an ornamental addition to human life, but an essential. A right relation to art is therefore one of those moral requirements with which the moral theologian and the priest must concern themselves. This does not, however, mean that they are competent to deliver professional judgments in the aesthetic sphere. For this reason we shall restrict ourselves to general observations.

Clearing out the Rubbish

Clearing out the rubbish is the first task. Anyone who has the gift of understanding and interpreting the language of art must unmask kitsch wherever it is to be found repressing spiritual life. Sometimes it is enough to expose it to ridicule. Occasionally more drastic action may be necessary, particularly against profiteers who see in kitsch an easy means of making money and who exploit it even to the point of blasphemy. Only public denunciation will help here, and the Catholic press ought not to neglect this necessary defence of public interest. Unsuspecting traders in devotional articles will certainly be impressed for their own good if a sufficient number of customers show unmistakably their contempt for the kitsch that is offered to them. In Germany, Catholic youth organizations have already done this successfully in some places.

It is even more important to clear the rubbish out of the soul of the Christian people; here it is necessary to proceed in a responsible and prudent way. We have already seen that for a limited time straightforward kitsch need not harm genuine religious sensitivity (pp. 68, 113) and that external symbols are necessary to man; inadequate forms of expression must therefore be tolerated until we can produce in their place a healthier art for general use which is also intelligible to ordinary people.

Education

Even so the educationalist and priest must work towards the rooting out of kitsch by unmasking its apparent harmlessness whenever they come across it. It is not a matter of taste which politeness forbids us to dispute, but a phenomenon of degeneration which dims, if it does not poison, religious life at its roots. The question should be raised at preparatory courses for marriage, in youth groups, sometimes even in the parochial sermon. The faithful ought to see that this is something which causes the priest acute pain in his pastoral, and not merely his aesthetic, sensitivity. Unfortunately the very opposite occurs; parishioners are reluctant to set about the necessary removal of rubbish from the church because the good parish priest so clings to the kitsch that is there. Is it his church or is it the house of God for the parish?

This raises the question whether training for the priesthood does not need some revision here. So long as people cannot distinguish between art and kitsch it is not enough that shops should stock the good with the bad. Kitsch is apt to have the more blatant appeal. We need much more aesthetic education. In England and in the United States since the war there has at least been a beginning in our general educational system. History of art is now a subject at more than one university, and through visual aids it is also beginning to be taught in schools. We need to apply this new spread of knowledge in the light of our Catholic faith; among alert and alive Christians the conviction must grow that by giving us the language of beauty, God made us a great gift, added another dimension to the good and the true, and endowed the world with new radiance. And that we need, therefore, to learn about this language. The artist by his nature has an almost priestly task. He must expose in the work of art, as in a monstrance, the intimations of God which are revealed to us in creation and in the Gospel. For the priest to deny himself the help of the beautiful is ungrateful and impious.

We live in a period when the eye seems more important than the brain, the picture more effective than the letter or the concept. It is useless to complain that spiritual values have been ousted by television, cinema and illustrated magazines; instead we need to make use of pictures in the right way. The National Catechetical Centre has made a beginning in England in this field.

It is not just kitsch-free homes which we need, but the cultivation of the capacity for experience and judgment in the aesthetic field, most of all in regard to the popular art which surrounds us. One method is by constant comparison, one work of art with another, the work of art with kitsch. Art should also be compared with the Christian truth or the historic reality which it expresses. Compare for instance a kitsch statue of St Anthony (Plate 25) with the authentic story of his life; it becomes obvious that this is not a symbol of the saint, but a mockery of him. We need also to recover the ability to understand and to experience religious symbolism. Christ himself spoke in picture and parable. These must be evaluated conceptually by the Church and protected in their content of truth by official teaching. But they must also remain alive in Christendom so that we can have some inkling of the depth and the vital necessity of this sort of truth. The symbolic language of art gives us such an inkling, and we know today once more how important it is for personal meditation to be directed not only to abstract truth and biblical parable, but also to the symbolism embodied in religious art.

A New Popular Art

What about the possibility of building up a new popular religious art? The first consideration must be a warning —hands off the creative artist. It should be common practice to commission works of art. In so doing we can provide for their production, but although we ought to discuss the questions involved and try mutually to seek a deeper understanding of the subjects chosen and the ways in which they may best be realized, we must leave the creative process untrammelled. What we have said at the beginning of this study about the process by which works of art come into being might help towards a sensitive appreciation of this and, indirectly, towards the unmasking of kitsch. But we must on no account regard this interpretation as some sort of rule which the artist in the midst of the creative process should keep before his eyes. Nor should priest and parish try to dictate their ideas so that the artist is forced to agree against his better judgment, because he has to live and probably also to support a family. He will of course approach his work with definite intentions; he may seek to edify, to give joy, naturally also to earn, but beyond this he must work freely, obedient only to his inner experience, to the demands of his inner imagery, wholly concerned with giving these artistic form. We hope that we have made it clear that art is not thereby placed beyond good and evil, but that these things rather make themselves felt in the human state and in the human behaviour of the artist during his artistic activity.

Plans, counsel, possibly also instruction and correction must be addressed to the man and the Christian in the artist. But in our well-meaning anxiety we must take care not to frustrate the artist's vitality, and above all we must remember that creative experience is a very different thing from the daily routine of office or bank. Finally, we must refrain from imposing moralistic restrictions on the artist's treatment of his subject. Art which tries to exclude evil and passion from its world on principle can scarcely be pleasing to God, because it must be untrue; what is important is that these elements should be in some way truly related to the positive order of things. It is in this way, not by turning its back on the evils of the world all around us, that art can help to overcome wickedness. Graham Sutherland's paintings of the Crucifixion at Northampton and Acton, for instance (Plate 26), are full of pain, ugliness, crudity; in our world of indifference to God, of cruelty and disillusion, can this crucial encounter between our Saviour and fallen mankind be truly depicted as something calmly triumphant? These pictures are about ourselves in relation to God, about the dilemma of modern man; the artist has penetrated through the surface of things to the raw reality, for him this finds expression in the pain, ugliness and crudity; and also in the immense power and vitality of the crucified figure.

Modern church building offers a unique opportunity not only of avoiding kitsch, but also of coming into vital and fruitful contact with all that is sound and holds promise for the future in modern art. Modern abstract art can also have its place in the church, for instance in stained-glass windows, vestments, etc. In this way the faithful can gain a truly spiritual profit from the impact of the contemporary world upon their habitual religious feelings. One has only to think of Coventry Cathedral and Ronchamp and an increasing number of modern churches all over the world and the impact which they make. It is relevant to remark also that the windows at Coventry, which are completely abstract in design, contribute a symbolism of colour which is immediately intelligible. Provided one looks at what is there—not for something that is not there—then the contrast of earthy and celestial colours spontaneously remind one of heaven and earth.

We have also to think of the modest tasks. In France especially attention has been drawn to the small steps which can be taken towards the renewal of religious art. It is in the domestic sphere, in which kitsch has flourished perhaps most luxuriantly, where it can most easily be fought so as to awaken the initiative of the average Christian. Why should people not try themselves to make the religious symbols which they need in their homes? If this is not possible, something may be achieved through direct contact with the religious artist. It is often just laziness or helplessness which leads to the purchase of the second best as presents, for children, etc. Catholic organizations, seminaries and convents could deal direct with individual artists, exchange ideas and state their needs. In every German diocese there is a priest in contact with artists who is able to make a bridge. Shops also could occasionally place a part of their window space at the disposal of individual artists or groups. In England we have the Guild of Catholic Artists, and the Visual Arts Week at Spode House. Where there is a will, there are many ways.

The Church is the Church of the people, of the poor in spirit, of the sinners, not of the perfect. This must be borne in mind also in relation to art. The Church is not concerned with highly cultured aesthetes, but with providing bread for thousands. Whenever a bishop or parish priest has the opportunity, he must make it his task to discover those masters who create with humility and love, who are able to clothe the holy in an exterior beauty which will be moving and meaningful for the ordinary Catholic. The flight to the past, an artificial reawakening of faded styles, possibly imposed with the aid of directives from the diocesan authorities, these are things which are an expression of the cultural destitution of the nineteenth century. Today the machine and modern techniques have taken the place of the handicrafts of the past, and these techniques have created new sorts of beauty which directly appeal to the modern man. To the youth of today which will seem the more relevant to life, and more beautiful, if put side by side, a modern car or a Lourdes grotto? If the latter is to be as meaningful as the former, it must somehow be put into equally contemporary terms. Our time offers promising opportunities; pastoral charity must seek them out and exploit them.

II

The Moral Approach

WE can and should also attack kitsch from the other side. Since kitsch is cheap, bogus and untrue, there must be something wrong with the part of us which likes kitsch, and this can be attacked at its source. Again, since kitsch falsifies true religion, then as we grow in true spiritual life we are bound to see through it in the end and reject it.

Since kitsch is bogus, the first antidote to oppose to it is the idea of genuineness, of responding truthfully to the situation of our life, trying to see both ourselves and the condition in which we find ourselves objectively. If we think of this ideal and then call to mind the kitsch hymns and pictures with which we are familiar, the discrepancy is glaring.

The taste for kitsch, as we have seen, is a sort of pleasure seeking; it is a taste for cosiness, a sort of sloth which is content to live in the narrow confined world of superficial experiences, which refuses therefore the real fullness of life. If we seek genuine life with courage, openness and an alert mind, kitsch will again appear in its true colours as spiritual dope.

Kitsch, as we have seen, both encourages the idea of a mass-produced, un-individualized sanctity, and also an individualistic type of devotion which isolates people from one another. Both these tendencies are opposed to the new sense of the Christian community which the liturgical revival and conciliar inspiration is promoting in England. The central fact of the Eucharistic meal which we are rediscovering demands outward forms which are worthy and expressive of the community. In so far as the sense of the Christian community grows, kitsch in vestments, hymns, ceremonies, and most of all on the altar, will appear extraneous and unworthy. As kitsch corresponds to mass-culture, so art corresponds to the community. A style which is truly characteristic of any period develops only where there is a living community; conversely, where there is a genuine community of spirit, in the long run this will find expression in a living art.

Fundamentally, kitsch is alien to Christianity as such. The fullness of truth and life which comes to us from divine revelation and grace contains an impressive motive power against kitsch. Basically, the position is quite simple; the Christian who is completely Christian down to the smallest details of his life will not be tempted by kitsch. But who can shape his life so thoroughly that he can penetrate even the most secret corners of his daily life? The most efficacious antidote is the New Testament; there is no kitsch in the words of our Lord or in the lives or writings of the apostles. A person who knows our Lord and follows him keeps his distance from kitsch. But anyone who knowingly offers to others the figure of Jesus in the distortion of kitsch is concealing Christ and scandalizing the little ones even though he seems to be making them happy. To sentimentalize and falsify the real image of the Saviour to innocent people is a scandal which may bring us under the condemnation of being drowned with a millstone round our necks in the depth of the sea. Nor will thoughtlessness and sloth free us from guilt if our naïve tastelessness and inattention have led to the entry of kitsch into the sanctuary. For anyone who has been confronted with our Lord in the Gospel, there can no longer be any invincible ignorance, no excuse of inculpable unawareness.

As well as the Gospel we have the theological teaching of the Church. God in the simplicity, fullness and clarity of his infinite Spirit is eternal beauty; all sense-bound beauty on earth can be called beautiful only by way of analogy. Of Divine Wisdom it is said in the Old Testament, "she is more beautiful than the sun . . . compared with the light, she is found before it" (Wisdom 7.29). The beauty of God, which is identical with himself, dwells for us in inaccessible light. Only "by the greatness and the beauty of the creature may the creator of them be seen" (Wisdom 13. 5). In the humanity of Christ we have had this shown to us in a unique way. All created beauty, therefore, is sacred, and for this reason we have to respect the value of the beautiful, and to strive to realize it, even though its fullness is unattainable to us.

This is true for us as God's creatures, but the Christian is more than this, for he knows that he possesses a new, supernatural sonship. The child resembles his father in a different way from the way in which the artist is resembled by his work. Because we became in Christ "sons in the Son" (Eckhart), we are also in Christ "the brightness of his glory and the figure of his substance" (Hebrews 1. 3). Through our incorporation by grace into the Word made flesh, now transfigured in glory, we have become ourselves the word of beauty which proclaims the eternal beauty of the Father. Sanctifying grace, the grace which makes holy, makes us beautiful in the same way that light gives beauty. But this was implanted in us at baptism only as a seed, and the effects of original sin conceal it as a dark veil; we have, therefore, to conform ourselves deliberately to the image of God, who is eternal beauty. How can it be right for a Christian to turn his back on this duty by conforming himself to a kitsch ideal? If the author of the Book of Wisdom long ago complained that men are by nature foolish and do not discover the divine artist by contemplating his works, how would he cry "woe" to those who cloud even the mirrors of earthly beauty with kitsch, and make it still more difficult for themselves and for those near to them to perceive the pure eternal beauty of God. Anyone, therefore, who has grasped at all the essential ordering of created beauty to God the Creator, will regard true beauty as a matter also of religious concern; he will set himself to seek and to grasp it, and if God has given him creative gifts, he will rejoice. The Christian ought to be revolted by kitsch, especially by religious kitsch, because this obscures the image of earthly beauty in the human art which ought to reflect it.

As Christians we have to accept our bodies and respect them more than other men do, because they are not only the creation of God, but temples of our redeemed souls and of the Holy Ghost. How can we "glorify God in our bodies", as St Paul bids us (1 Cor. 6. 19), when in religious kitsch it is precisely the corporeal-sensible element which is degraded to unworthy ends and is no longer transparent of the holy—when, indeed, the holy is irreverently made a pretext for all-too-human interests?

God has chosen to nourish our bodies with the flesh of the divine Redeemer, they are consecrated in the sacramental mystery and the *fervor caritatis*, the ardour of the love of God roused by the Holy Spirit flows over them. How then can we think that the "embodying" of the holy in religious art can be dismissed as an inessential trimming in religious life, or still more that there can be any excuse for allowing this embodiment to be prevented by the substitution of kitsch?

Again, because we live in the body, God in his goodness

has given us the sacraments; thus the symbolism of all created things is ennobled. For the sacraments effect what they signify and they symbolize the life of grace, the participation in the life of the triune God. The Church has incorporated the administration of the sacraments into the holy play of the liturgy, and so both enhanced and fulfilled their essential claim to a worthy and beautiful outward form. Through this liturgical play, through the holy signs of the sacraments, all created things regain their symbolic character and their deeper reality; we learn to stop looking at things superficially, to stop rating them for their usefulness alone; seeing them as symbols, we perceive beyond their outward beauty the more sublime beauty of the spiritual. Under the influence of this experience, the temptation to dwell on kitsch in an atmosphere of sensual pleasure is driven out by a real joy in the experience of beauty seen as an aspect of the sacramental Christian life.

Modern man has seen too much suffering, and knows too well how he is threatened by the powers of darkness to consider that the ideal of a beautiful peacefully devout life is relevant to the world in which he lives. We have to remember that though Christ has risen and is enthroned in radiant beauty at the right hand of the Father, that though everyone who is saved has in his soul by grace a share in this transfigured beauty, for us this beauty has become real and important through the Cross. Our Saviour is the Crucified, in whom there was no longer "beauty or comeliness" (Isaiah 53.2). It is not art which redeems, but self-sacrificing love. We cannot expect to see ideal beauty, or to experience it in an effortless, painless way; we must not try to anticipate the transfigured beauty which is not of this world. For one who lives in Christ because he has died with him, all that is beautiful becomes attainable and capable of being given expression only through the Cross. The Cross is a filter which lets through the pure and the beautiful, and separates out the kitsch. In brief, all artistic and worthy expression of the religious life must have the character of a sacrifice, and to the extent that our religious life becomes a sacrifice and an expression of selfless devotion to the Father in Jesus Christ, it will be beautiful, and remain free from the falsification of kitsch. We have to face the heights and the depths of human life, we have to live in the Lord, then necessarily we must see through the cheapness, the shoddiness, the untruthfulness of kitsch.

Epilogue: Kitsch in England Today

No one can question that Catholic churches, convents, schools, homes in England are full of kitsch, or that we are often asked to sing kitsch hymns. To our shame kitsch statues and pictures might be said to be the distinguishing mark of the contemporary Catholic church as seen by the casual visitor, and kitsch devotional articles are often on sale in the church porch. What a contrast is this with the record of the Church through the ages; until recently she has always been the great patron of artists and the builder of the great cathedrals; she has always taught that we should offer to God the best of the work of our hands, and in so doing has inspired very many of the very greatest works of the imagination. Why is it that this kitsch is now tolerated? What reasons are given by priests and educated Catholics?

Some say that they like these hymns and images; or is it perhaps that they have never really thought about them, but simply accepted them as part of the Church? For such people this book surely provides much material for thought.

Some say, "It is just a matter of taste; you dislike these things, other people like them. Why should you think that your opinion is more important than theirs?" But it is not just my opinion. It is the unanimous opinion of everyone who loves art or has studied it, that the "art" illustrated in Plates 1, 11, 12, 17, 20, is about as low as artefacts can sink; that it is slovenly and unskilled, and completely out of touch with the contemporary world. Outside the Church, the remark quoted above would in this context seem fantastic to any educated person; art, like science or theology, or any other human activity, is a field where aptitude, experience and study are valuable. Is it not ignorance and foolishness to think that the opinion of those who have such qualifications is to be valued no more than the opinion of those who have no qualifications? In fact, this is at bottom an obscurist, anti-intellectual attitude.

Some say, "I know these things are awful, but the people like them, and why should they not have what they like?" This question Professor Egenter has answered in the most unequivocal terms. The choice between good and bad art is not one which is morally indifferent; bad art corrupts moral and spiritual life as well as taste.

Some again say, "The great thing about this stuff is that it is cheap and anyone can afford it". Would the people who are thought to need such cheap crucifixes give their children a doll of similar quality, coarsely moulded in plastic, with red carelessly smeared on to show the blood which bought our salvation? Does it not teach people to think cheaply of our Lord even, if they are told that rubbishy emblems such as these are good enough? Devotional articles must be almost the cheapest quality goods that people buy today; in our affluent society, surely it would show a truer scale of values if we were asked to save, at least for a week or two, a few pounds, instead of shillings, and so buy something which, at the very least, is of decent workmanship and material. If we are really poor, is a plain cross not more reverent and more prayer-inspiring than a cheap figure of our Lord? The literal cheapness of the "art" offered to Catholics in England is one of the worst aspects of our kitsch. Nothing can survive it; I have seen a reproduction of Michelangelo's wonderful Pietà in St Peter's, which he carved with such exquisite feeling and delicacy, reduced to a parody, shrivelled and coarsened almost out of recognition. Old master paintings are sometimes reproduced in such crude and untrue colours, and printed in such careless register that they too are almost unrecognizable (sold also without acknowledgment to the artist). One cannot but be aware that the makers of these things obviously think that they are not worth careful reproduction, their first consideration is cheapness; the quality of these things is in fact dictated by commercial incentives. To say that people must be supplied with cheap religious art is to promote this type of thing.

Then there are educated people, even art-loving people, who say that they like kitsch in church, that anyhow they do not think that it should be fought against. Sometimes this is the feeling of the convert who has felt that this was something that he had to accept with the Church, who perhaps made an act of humility in mastering his repugnance to these things, a repugnance which perhaps he interpreted as a sort of intellectual arrogance; and so has come in a way to love that which he originally found a stumbling-block. Partly perhaps it is that we have so often met good and holy people who really seemed to think these things beautiful, and so we have lacked the courage, or it seemed too rude, too unheard of, to protest; and so we have got used to accepting the situation, and so it has all grown rather cosy. This is the Church, where we are at home, not a refined, tasteful, Sundays-only place, but crude and human, taking people for what they are. But the kitsch statues do not however, as Professor Egenter has shown, represent life as it is, still less God as he is. Must bad taste and meanness be the dominant characteristic of the visual image of the modern Church to the world, and to the children growing up within it? If the Church is poor, would not austerity be better than kitsch? We are being woken up out of our cosy devotional life by the new liturgy; is not this another outward form of the spiritual life of the Church where there is a crying need for a parallel renewal?

One of the most terrifying features of our kitsch is the extent to which we feed our children upon it. It is offered to them in church, in first-communion souvenirs and prayer books, at school in filmstrips and other visual aids, on the classroom walls, in comics and children's books, everywhere where they meet the Church; in the crude drawing and bogus historical "realism" of illustrations to the Gospel stories, in emasculated images of saints and angels, and in the image of Christ. Is there any Catholic in England who has not got that typical visual image of the "Sacred Heart" indelibly printed on his mind as an idea of God incarnate? And in what way does it correspond to any truth of God as Love, or have any relevance to life as it has to be lived? Is it surprising that a child who thinks that God is like that should, as he grows up, reject the reality of such a figure? The Church has always used outward signs, every form of visual aid, to teach her members about God. Through a traditional symbolism which is particularly memorable, pictures, poetry, music give us knowledge of God. Professor Egenter has shown that the basic characteristic of kitsch is that it is bogus, untrue. Does it not follow that to offer children religious kitsch is to give them a false idea of God and religion? And that is what we do offer them *almost exclusively*.

The last answer which people have given to me as a reason for maintaining kitsch is, "What can we have instead?" We have been saying for so long that we have no religious art, that it offers almost insoluble problems, when people have merely forgotten to notice how—thanks largely to the faith and courage of a few patrons, mostly non-Catholic—a very remarkable living religious art has been growing up in our midst.

The greatest of the problems facing a modern religious artist has been our loss of a sense of symbolism. Symbols have come to be things that have to be learnt; not as they should be, signs with immediate, indestructible connotations. The cross has perhaps always remained such a symbol, but the heart for instance—though verbally it conveys emotion-feeling-love—is visually only the symbol of a physical organ; which is why most of us are instinctively physically repulsed by seeing it represented on top of pseudo-realistic clothes, particularly so if it is also crowned with thorns. For this reason, because the popular devotion is nineteenth century, a time when symbolism was no longer a current way of thought, most genuine artists have found it impossible to find any visual image for the Sacred Heart. Yet all art is necessarily in some way symbolic— an expression (and communication) of an immaterial idea or experience in sensible form. In particular this must apply to religious art which specifically deals with religious truths, and which in so far as it illustrates the Gospel story has somehow to convey the figure of Christ as God as well as man. In the early Middle Ages this could be done by any artist by the simple expedient of making this figure larger in scale than his companions. With the Renaissance came both the revival of the classical illusionist tradition in art and the new scientific interest in the natural world; the artist started from the new point of view that the outward aspect of things was a true indication of their total reality and the science of perspective localized the subject in a particular moment of space and time. The divinity of Christ, and the supra-temporal significance of the events of his life could therefore only be conveyed by the sheer intensity of the individual artist's conception. It is a telling indication of the crucial importance of the artist's intention, and also of his power to get this over to the beholder, that most Christian pictures do manage in some degree to get this over—this was brought home to me the other day when I saw a popular religious print (not in a Catholic shop) and realized with a shock that what was wrong with it (among other things) was that the artist had thought of our Lord simply as a "good man". The greatest artists, such as Piero della Francesca or Michelangelo, convey the spiritual reality of the Christian message as forcibly as does the Byzantine Pantocrator, but lesser artists of the Renaissance tradition, using as they must the patterns and types evolved by other more creative minds, often lack this intensity of conception; they can only inform these borrowed outward patterns with trivial or sentimental or dishonest feeling and so kitsch creeps in. The Romanesque artist or one working in the Byzantine tradition could produce bad work, crude, even dead work, but because he worked in a symbolic tradition, when he lacks artistic gifts his product lapses into a mere symbol, without aesthetic life, not into kitsch. In the realistic tradition, on the other hand, it is almost inevitable that the stylistic derivation of the worst kitsch should go back to the greatest masters.

In the Catholic countries of Europe, the Renaissance was followed by the ecstatic-sensuous baroque-rococo tradition in religious art described by Professor Egenter. In England there was no such interlude. Apart from a few dreary altarpieces by Benjamin West (and the Infant Samuel—Plate 10), there is hardly any religious painting in England until the nineteenth century, until Blake, Dyce and the Pre-Raphaelites. Blake invented his own symbolism, and to some extent carries it over by sheer force of genius, but its frame of reference is to his own myth rather than to the Christian faith. His followers in the romantic mood, John Martin and Doré, did certainly manage in their Old Testament illustrations to give a vivid sense of supra-mundane apocalyptic events, but neither had the aesthetic gifts to match their grandiose conceptions, and neither was equal to New Testament scenes. Dyce followed the Nazarenes of a generation earlier. The great Victorian religious artists were Holman Hunt (Plate 14), Ford Madox Brown, and the young Millais. For them renaissance realism was the true vision, neither the baroque tradition nor eighteenth-century English academic ideas of ideal types seemed meaningful, and unlike the German Nazarenes they did not lapse into an archaic dream world. They tried to follow an absolutely honest and contemporary vision, in harmony with the dynamic scientific thought of their time, "to envisage events as they must have happened". *Christ in the Carpenter's Shop* and Ford's *Christ washing the feet of St Peter* are for instance paintings of sincerity and vision. But the movement found itself between two difficulties. Holman Hunt, who was the one artist who devoted himself throughout his life to religious subjects, as we have already seen (p. 47), became involved in the contradiction between the symbolism in his thought and the realism of his theory of painting, and failed to find a real solution. The obvious Victorian answer was to concentrate on "events as they must have happened", to read history, to follow biblical research, to study Roman and oriental remains, and to go to the Holy Land in order to recover the biblical atmosphere and to realize its setting. It all sounds so right; it was certainly done by more than one artist in great sincerity. And yet the results were unsuccessful, and ultimately—indeed rather speedily—led to kitsch. Today surely we know the reason, because we have a less simplified view of history and of biblical scholarship. Professor Gombrich in his *Art and Illusion* starts off by pointing out how at different periods people have drawn pictures of themselves, and each drawn them quite differently. The Victorians drew the people of the past in what they thought was the only true way of drawing—but the results are not a living creation of the past, but pictures of Victorians dressed up. Today we are more ready to think that when the Normans and Anglo-Saxons, for instance, drew themselves in manuscripts or in the Bayeux Tapestry, they drew a "truer" picture than anything that we can reconstruct. They were different from us, not because they wore different clothes, but because they thought differently. The first-century—and Old Testament—Jews made no pictures, even had they done so it would not help us; no one can draw in the idiom of another time. In fact the only true historical picture that we can form of the past must be based on an acceptance of the fact that we see it with the eyes of the present. The idea that we can see it objectively "as it must have happened" is a delusion. This delusion bedevilled late Victorian religious art. Greater artists would no doubt have managed to break through the unreality, but they were not forthcoming. And so the genuine attempts of Holman Hunt and his contemporaries only made the way easier for kitsch for Northern kitsch stemming from Thorvaldsen, the Nazarenes, Peter von Cornelius, etc. (in any case a powerful stylistic influence in English nineteenth-century painting), and later for French kitsch which had the prestige of being Catholic, and which was so closely connected with the cult of Lourdes and the Little Flower.

The late Victorians failed, but twentieth-century English artists have gone on searching for means to express in visual terms the living reality of Christianity. If it is unreal to paint the past in fancy dress, if as experience shows only too forcefully this makes it less, not more, real, the logical thing is to paint in modern dress. Stanley Spencer, Carol Weight and other modern artists have done this, and the results are certainly the beginning of a new sense of Christ in our midst today, even if to some extent this seems private to the artist, rather than an expression of a common faith. Certainly the modern sense of history is so ingrained that this solution tends to seem forced.

Another solution has been to try to turn back and pick up the stream of Catholic art before the sense of symbolism was lost. The art of the past is part of our inheritance, part of the Church; it enormously enlarges our understanding of the Faith. Professor Southern has a very illuminating passage in *The Making of the Middle Ages*, in which he explains how the early Romanesque crucifix reflects the contemporary theology which saw the Redemption as the triumphant climax of the fight between God and the devil, in which man was the helpless spectator of a cosmic struggle, the Cross *vexilla regis*, Christ the victor-hero, crowned and God-like; how this was gradually replaced, under the influence of St Anselm, St Bernard and St Francis, by a new image of Christ our fellow-man, and the growth of new compassion in his sufferings which found expression in the tenderness and realism of the Gothic crucifix. The comparison could easily be carried on; one has only to think of the conceptions of Grünewald, Masaccio, Rubens, El Greco, Rembrandt, to recall the wonderful range of vision, the new dimensions of understanding, which the art of the past makes available to us. All this is our inheritance, and we should use it all. But to reinhabit any particular period, if only for the reason that we cannot cut out of our minds what has happened in between, is not possible. The archaism of Eric Gill seems on the whole to lead to emptiness; the work of his followers is apt to be weak, but it is good workmanship and sincere: a great break at the least from kitsch. A more recent development along rather the same line is the new style in children's book illustration which seems to be international, as represented by the Dove books (Plate 24) and those of the Benedictines of Cockfosters. Romanesque influence has been reinforced by that of children's drawings, with their apparently innate symbolism; it seems a more basic starting-point, provided it develops and does not degenerate into infantilism.

Meanwhile, the whole idea of realistic art has been shattered. The advent of photography has called in question the purpose of art; the psychology of perception has made us rethink the aesthetics of illusionism, modern science has demonstrated the unreality of appearances. And the *avant garde* artists have all the time been testing, searching, creating new standards of vision, discarding those no longer valid and seeking new forms uncluttered with associations which are no longer meaningful. They are seeking, in fact, means of communication which are true and unequivocal to the artist and to the beholder. It is not surprising that the modern movement has found it necessary to explore to the bedrock of visual forms. One of the basic discoveries has been that of the validity of visual symbolism; Kandinsky's book *Concerning the Spiritual in Art* is a classic statement. Today art is free. The artist can use what terms he feels necessary, and these are understood by an ever growing number of people, who are used to "reading" the sophisticated semi-abstract language of, for instance, the modern advertisement. He is understood in quite a different way from the way in which the traditional kitsch Catholic art is understood, because the new art language is alive, unquestionably belonging to our time.

The modern Catholic artist has not necessarily been forced down to the bedrock (or into the freedom) of abstract art in order to communicate. For him the outward forms of the world have to a greater or less degree, remained meaningful through his faith, while the modern movement to which he also belongs has given him also the new freedom. He can use colour and line and form for what they are and no more—line which moves or divides, burning scarlet, or translucent blue or the black of night, forms which are stable, dancing, nebulous; he can delineate human forms without having to detail their clothes or materialize their whereabouts—it is in the painting that they have their existence, between the artist and the beholder. Plate 27 shows a successful contemporary use of symbolism.

When we come to think it over, the religious artists of this century, in England alone, are of remarkable stature. Eric Gill's *Stations of the Cross* in Westminster Cathedral, Jacob Epstein's *Madonna* at Cavendish Square and his Lazarus in New College, Oxford, Stanley Spencer's *Resurrection*, and Burghclere Chapel, John Piper's windows at Eton (Plate 27), Oundle and Coventry, Evie Hone's windows at Eton and Farm Street, Ceri Richards' *Supper at Emmanus* at St Edmund Hall, Graham Sutherland's *Crucifixions* at Northampton and Acton, his Christ at Coventry and *Noli me Tangere* at Chichester, David Jones's inscriptions, his *Agnus Dei* and *Vexilla Regis*, Elizabeth Frink's *The Risen Christ* (Plate 28); to name only a few major works which have been made this century, constitute a list of which we may well be proud. It far outshines any other country since the death of Rembrandt.

Epilogue

And yet we still buy and sell and live with kitsch. Not only the old kitsch which is not even the product of our own tradition, but new kitsch like Plate 12 of the pin-up, film star type, and Plate 17 which pretends to be modern, but actually consists of a meaningless simplification which reduces the human form to a boneless, faceless, shapeless pattern. To leave a face undefined can be nearer to reality than an inadequate naturalistic conception; after all, the only things that the Gospels tell us about the appearance of our Lord and our Lady are that he was not recognized on two occasions. That the beholder should draw on his own imagination, co-operate with the artist in his attempt to visualize the Gospel story is appropriate. We needed to abandon realistic representation because it obscured the spiritual, in order to put more meaning, more life into art. But in this case there has been no such intention: the abandonment of realism has merely provided the artist with an excuse for not troubling to draw or bothering to think. That there should be a sale for these two types of object seems a confirmation of Professor Egenter's thesis that the habit of kitsch corrupts. In a different category are the works of Dali (Plates 6 and 7). These are not cheap and shoddy, but very expensive and very accomplished, and for that reason more insidious; these to my mind are evil kitsch. Yet there are already, or there could easily be made, substitutes for these things. Cheap reproductions are kitsch, but if a work is designed for reproduction, there is no question of losing the immediacy of the artist's personal touch, because it will not have been conceived in that way. So modern techniques and materials can be used to make new things to the glory of God instead of debasing old ones. It is up to us, the purchasers, to reject kitsch root and branch, and to make our contribution to the living contemporary Catholic art of our country.